From Chaos to Harmony

The Solution to the Global Crisis According to the Wisdom of Kabbalah

LAITMAN
KABBALAH PUBLISHERS

Rav Michael Laitman, PhD

FROM CHAOS TO HARMONY
The Solution to the Global Crisis According to the Wisdom of Kabbalah

Copyright © 2006 by MICHAEL LAITMAN

All rights reserved
Published by Laitman Kabbalah Publishers
www.kabbalah.info   info@kabbalah.info
1057 Steeles Avenue West, Suite 532, Toronto, ON, M2R 3X1, Canada
194 Quentin Rd, 2nd floor, Brooklyn, New York, 11223, USA

Printed in Canada

Library of Congress Cataloging-in-Publication Data
Laitman, Michael.
From chaos to harmony:
the solution to the global crisis according to the wisdom of Kabbalah /
Michael Laitman; [translation, Chaim Ratz]. — 1st ed.
p. cm.
Includes bibliographical references.
ISBN 0-9781590-4-7
1. Cabala. 2. Mysticism—Judaism. 3. Spiritual life—Judaism.
4. Self-actualization (Psychology)—Religious aspects—Judaism.
5. Nature—Religious aspects—Judaism. 6. World politics.
7. Conduct of life. I. Title.
BM525.L2477 2007
296.7—dc22   2006035132

Translation: Chaim Ratz
Copy Editor: Claire Gerus
Layout: Baruch Khovov
Cover Design: Richard Aquan
Printing and Post Production: Uri Laitman
Executive Editor: Oren Levi

FIRST EDITION: FEBRUARY 2007

From Chaos to Harmony
TABLE OF CONTENTS

About The Author

Kabbalist Rav Michael Laitman, PhD, has a doctorate in philosophy and Kabbalah from the High Institute of Philosophy at the Russian Academy of Sciences in Moscow, and an MSc in bio-cybernetics from the Faculty of Biology and Cybernetics at the Institute of Science at St. Petersburg University.

In addition to his work as a scientist and a researcher, Rav Laitman has been studying and teaching Kabbalah for the past thirty years. As a Kabbalist, he has published more than thirty books and numerous academic essays on the subject, which have been translated into ten languages thus far.

Rav Laitman was the disciple and personal assistant of Rabbi Baruch Shalom HaLevi Ashlag (the Rabash), the firstborn and successor of Rabbi Yehuda Leib HaLevi Ashlag, known as Baal HaSulam (Owner of the Ladder) for authoring the *Sulam* (Ladder) commentary on *The Book of Zohar*. For twelve years, Rav Laitman devotedly studied with the Rabash, and absorbed from him the teachings of Baal HaSulam.

Baal HaSulam is considered the successor of the Holy Ari, author of *The Tree of Life*. Yehuda Ashlag also paved the way for our generation to be admitted into Kabbalah. Thanks to his methodology, anyone can benefit from the knowledge within the (authentic sources of) Kabbalah, the legacy of the ancient Kabbalists.

Rav Laitman follows in the footsteps of his mentor and continues to fulfill his life's mission: disseminating the wisdom of Kabbalah to the world. After the Rabash's demise in 1991, Laitman established Bnei Baruch, a group of Kabbalah students that studies, teaches, and implements the teachings of Baal HaSulam and his son, Baruch, on a daily basis.

Over time, Bnei Baruch has grown into an extensive international movement with thousands of members in Israel and around the world. Rav Laitman's lectures are broadcast live daily on satellite and cable TV in Israel, in the U.S., and on the Internet at www.kab.tv.

Additionally, Laitman is founder and president of the Ashlag Research Institute (ARI), whose goal is to cultivate open discourse about Kabbalah and science. His extensive educational activities awarded him the title Professor of Ontology from the Russian Academy of Sciences in Moscow. In recent years, Rav Laitman has been cooperating with leading scientists in research concerning Kabbalah and contemporary science.

When asked how he fits both Kabbalah and science into his life, he replied:

"When I finished high school, I looked for a profession that would allow me to research the meaning of life. I felt that studying Nature through a scientific lens would help me find the answer. This is why I began to study Bio-cybernetics, a field of knowledge that researches life's systems and the order that dictates their existence. I had hoped that by studying how we live, I would eventually find what we are living for. This is a question that finds its way into the heart of every young person, but dissipates in the rat race of day-by-day living.

"When I concluded my studies, I took a job at the Institute of Hematology Research in Leningrad. Even as a student, I was in awe of how organic cells sustain life, and how each cell is perfectly integrated in the whole body. It is customary to research cell structure itself and its different functions, and ask about the purpose of its existence and how its actions relate to the whole organism. However, I could not find an answer to my question about the purpose of the existence of the whole organism.

"I assumed that the body, like the cells within it, is part of a greater whole. But my attempts to research this hypothesis were repeatedly turned down. I was told that science does not engage in these questions.

"All this happened in the 1970's in Russia. Disillusioned, I decided to leave Russia as quickly as I could. I had hoped to be able to continue the research that so captured my heart in Israel. And thus, in 1974, after being a "refusenik" (one whose request to leave Russia for Israel is refused) for four years, I finally arrived in Israel. Alas, even here I was only allowed to engage in research that was limited to the single cell level.

"I realized I had to look elsewhere for a place to learn about the overall systems of reality. Consequently, I turned to philosophy, then to religion, but found answers in neither. Only after long years of searching did I find my teacher. It was the great Kabbalist, Rabbi Baruch Shalom HaLevi Ashlag (the Rabash).

"I spent the next twelve years alongside the Rabash, from 1979 to 1991. To me he was "the last of the Mohicans," the last great Kabbalist in the great dynasty of Kabbalists that endured for many generations. I did not move from his side that whole time; I wrote my first three books in 1983 with his support, and when he passed away, I began to develop the knowledge I had received from him, and to publish it. I considered this work then, as I do now, a direct extension of Rabash's way and the realization of his vision."

THE STRUCTURE
OF THE BOOK

This book is based on essays and lectures given by Rav Michael Laitman, PhD, which were then edited by staff members of the Ashlag Research Institute (ARI). The first part, "From Chaos to Harmony," focuses on the personal level. It explains the root of every crisis and predicament we experience in life, and depicts how we can resolve them. The second part of the book is dedicated to the future of the state of Israel.

FOREWORD

It is hardly a secret that humanity is in a deep crisis. Many of us already feel it. Sensations of meaninglessness, frustration, and emptiness engulf our lives. Family crises, a troubled educational system, drug abuse, personal insecurities, and fear of nuclear war and ecological threats, all cloud our happiness. It seems we have lost control of our lives and are unable to head off problems as they unfold.

It is common knowledge that correctly diagnosing an illness is half its cure. Hence, to resolve our problems, we first need to understand their causes. The safest place to start is by understanding human nature and the nature of the world. If we understand our own nature and the laws affecting us, we will know where we are erring and what we must do to end the predicament we're in.

When we observe our surrounding Nature, we discover that the inanimate, vegetative, and animate levels
of Nature are all driven by inherent instincts. These actions are not considered good or bad; they simply follow
the rules imbued within them, in harmony with Nature
and with each other.

However, if we observe man's nature, we will find
that it is essentially different from the rest of Nature.
Man is the only creature that can take pleasure in exploit-
ing others and in seeking sovereignty over another. Only
man receives pleasure from being unique, apart from,
and superior to others. Thus, man's egoism breaches
Nature's balance.

The desire to receive pleasure evolved in us over time,
following the growth of human desires. Its first manifestation was in simple desires, such as wanting to eat, to
reproduce, and to experience family. The appearance of
more advanced desires, such as craving wealth, honor,
sovereignty, and knowledge, prompted the evolution of
human society and its social structures: education, culture, science, and technology. Humanity marched proud-
ly forward, believing that progress and economic growth
would satisfy us and make us happier. Alas, today we are
beginning to realize that this protracted "evolution" has
reached a standstill.

The reason for this is that our desire to receive pleasure cannot remain satisfied for long. We've all, at least
once, wanted something very badly, sometimes for years.
But once we received what we wanted, the pleasure faded

shortly afterward, the emptiness returned and we found ourselves chasing new goals, hoping they would give us satisfaction. This process occurs on both the individual level and on the level of all humanity.

Now that we have accumulated experience for thousands of years, we realize that we don't know how to reach sustainable happiness, or even basic inner security. We are bewildered. This phenomenon is at the basis of the crises and the challenges that plague us.

Moreover, the natural, egoistic human predilection to seek self-centered pleasures at the expense of others has intensified over time. Today, people are trying to build their successes on the ruin of others. Intolerance, alienation, and hatred have reached new and terrifying heights, jeopardizing the very existence of the human species.

When we observe Nature, we see that all living creatures are built to follow the principle of altruism, or caring for others. This is a fundamentally different principle from the one that motivates humans.

Cells in organisms unite by reciprocal giving for the sake of sustaining the whole body. Each cell in the body receives what it needs for its sustenance, and spends the rest of its energy tending to the rest of the body. At every level of Nature, the individual works to benefit the whole of which it is part, and in that finds its wholeness. Without altruistic activities, a body cannot persist. In fact, life *itself* cannot persist.

Today, after researching many different fields, science is arriving at the conclusion that humanity, too, is actually one whole body. The problem is, we human beings are still unaware of it. We must wake up and understand that the problems that cloud our present lives are not coincidental; they cannot be resolved by any means that we know from the past. They will not stop, but will worsen until we change direction and begin to function in accord with the comprehensive law of Nature—the law of altruism.

Every negative phenomenon in our lives, from the most specific to the most general, stems from disobeying Nature's law. If we jump off a high place and are harmed, we know we acted against the law of gravity. Thus, today we must stop and examine ourselves to see where we are not following Nature's law. We must find the right way of life. It all depends on our awareness: the better we understand Nature's system, the less suffering we will experience, and the faster we will evolve.

At the animate level, altruism is the law of existence. But at the human level, we ourselves must build this kind of relationship. Nature has left it for us so that we can elevate ourselves to a new and exalted level of existence. This is the essential difference between man and all other creatures.

In this book, we will discuss how to implement altruistic relationships, since it is no small task to change human Nature. We were created as egoists, and we cannot go directly against our ego, as it is our Nature. So the "trick" is to find a method that can make each of us *egoistically* want to change our attitude to others, to bond to one another as parts of a single body.

It is not by chance that Nature created us as social beings. If we look deep into our behavior, we will find that every action we take is intended to bring us society's appreciation. This is what sustains us, and its absence or, worse, the denunciation of society, causes us the greatest suffering.

Being shamed is the most terrible thing a person can experience. This is why we tend to abide by the values that society places before us. Thus, if we succeed in changing the values of the environment we live in, bringing altruistic values such as caring for others, sharing, and bonding to the top of the ladder, we can then change our attitudes toward others.

When society values a person solely by his or her devotion to society, we will all necessarily strive to think and to act in favor of society. If we eliminate the awards we give for individual excellence, and appreciate people only for their concern for society, if children judge their parents by these standards, if friends, relatives, and colleagues examine us only according to how well we relate to others, we will all want to do good to others so we can win society's appreciation.

Thus, we will gradually come to feel that expressing altruism, or unselfishness, toward others is a special and sublime value in and of itself, regardless of the social recognition it grants. In doing so, we will find that this attitude is actually a source of perfect and unbounded pleasure.

Even though today's society is egoistic, it is quite prepared to advance toward following Nature's law of altruism. Education and culture have always been established on altruistic principles. In our homes and at school, we teach our children to be compassionate, kind, friendly. We want our children to be nice to others, and we feel that such an attitude toward others is the proper way, and that it protects those who follow it. Hardly anyone would declare opposition to these values.

Additionally, thanks to the progress in communication, today we can transmit new messages and values to society very quickly throughout the world. This is a crucial factor in increasing the awareness of humankind's escalating crisis and the need for a comprehensive resolution.

Although our current problems may be prompting us to change, there is more to it than that. When we build a correct attitude toward society, we are gradually admitted into a whole new level of existence, superior to anything we've known before. It is a higher form of existence, supernal, a sensation of Nature's wholeness and perfection.

Now, after numerous generations of evolution, we have accumulated sufficient experience to understand where Nature's evolutionary law is leading us.

The picture we will gradually present to the reader is founded on principles from the ancient wisdom of Kabbalah, along with contemporary science's latest discoveries. This book is intended to teach us how to re-solve the crisis, and pave a way to prosperity and success. With it, we will be able to take our first real steps toward realizing Nature's law. Only then can we feel we are all part of Nature's single, comprehensive system, and taste the perfection and harmony within it.

PART ONE

From Chaos
to Harmony

PROLOGUE

The first part of this book will focus on humanity's state in the 21st century, describing what change is required in our awareness, and why it is needed. But before we do that, let's review some facts about humankind's present state, focusing on the situation in Israel. Knowing these facts is important to help us understand the proposed solution to our problems.

In the last 100 years or so, we have made a giant leap in scientific and technological progress, and yet we find ourselves helpless and perplexed in the face of escalating phenomena in many areas. Many of us are dissatisfied with our lives, and there is a growing sense of insecurity, meaninglessness, frustration, and bitterness. These sensations often lead to our using sedatives, drugs and other additions, all serving as substitutes and alternative means of fulfillment.

The plagues of the 21st century are anxiety and depression. The World Health Organization (WHO) has determined that every fourth person will suffer from a mental problem during his or her life.[1] Over the past fifty years, there has been a significant increase in the number of people suffering from depression. The newest finding is that depression appears at younger and younger ages. It is anticipated that by the year 2020, mental ailments, and primarily depression, will be the second most common cause of health problems.

Depression is one of the prime causes of suicide. Each year, more than a million people will take their own lives, and between 10 and 20 million people will attempt it.[2] Suicide attempts in general, and particularly among children and youth, are on a clear upward curve.

The Israeli Ministry of Health declared that in Israel, similar to other Western developed countries, suicides are the second most common cause of death among children and youth.[3] Many among those who work in the health field believe that the suicide phenomenon reflects the overall unhealthy state of society.

In the last decades, drug intake has turned from a marginal phenomenon to a central issue the world over, and today, every level of society is affected by it. Drug abuse among youth is a familiar phenomenon today, and children are introduced to drugs as early in life as elementary school. A 2005 survey conducted by Israel

Anti-Drug Authority revealed that compared to past data, there is an alarming amount of drug abuse among young people.

In the U.S., the number of people who confess to using drugs at least once during their lives is approximately 42% of the overall population.[4] In Europe, consumption of cocaine has reached an unsettling record high of 3.5 million users, among which are increasing numbers of highly educated people from the Western part of the continent.[5]

Even the family institution is in decline: divorce, alienation, and domestic violence are appearing far more frequently. In Israel, every third couple divorces; in Sweden and in Russia, divorce occurs in 65% of the couples.[6] The Israeli police reported that in 2004, 9,400 new cases were opened against parents abusing their children, compared to 1,000 in 1998. Additionally, in 2004, 200,000 women were classified as victims of domestic violence inflicted by their partners.[7]

The poverty report published by the Israeli Social Security in 2006 revealed that expansion of poverty and socioeconomic gaps is continuing. Today, every third child grows up in a poor family, and every fifth family in Israel lives below the poverty line.

The younger generation suffers from an absence of values and ideology, and the education system is helpless and in decline. Violence and juvenile delinquency are on the rise, and 90% of the students report witnessing regular harassment and violence within school premises.

A similar percentage of the teachers admit that they haven't the means to cope with the violence and insubordination within the education system.

In fact, the intensification of these phenomena is not so disturbing in our eyes because we have grown accustomed to them. In the past, they were considered aberrant, but today they have become the norm. Because we lack the tools to cope with these predicaments, we accept their existence to reduce the suffering they cause us. This is a natural defense mechanism that has developed within us, but it does not mean that things cannot be different, and indeed better than they are now.

                                                    --The Editor

1

DESIRE IS EVERYTHING

ONE CAUSE, ONE SOLUTION

As we have written in the foreword, many of us already feel there is an unfolding crisis on the global and on the personal levels. As a matter of fact, it encompasses the whole of Nature: still, vegetative, animate, and the human society. Hence, it is not enough to tend to specific areas; we are required to locate the root of the problems and attend to correcting them.

This part of the book will show that there is a single reason behind all the negative phenomena. When we understand that reason, we will be able to provide a single, comprehensive resolution.

We will begin with our knowledge of human nature and the Nature of the world. If we acquire a better understanding of these, with all their rules and facets, we will be able to see where we are erring. Thus, we will also be able to first end the predicaments in our lives, and subsequently advance toward a much brighter future.

Studying various substances reveals that the primal desire of all matter and every object is to preserve its existence. Yet, this focus is expressed differently in each substance. Solid objects have a shape that is fixed and defined, making it difficult to penetrate their "boundaries," while other forms guard themselves by movement and change. Thus, we must ask ourselves what makes each substance behave in a certain manner and be separated from other materials? What is it that dictates the actions of each form of matter?

The behavior of substances is somewhat similar to a computer screen. We may be impressed with the picture on the screen, but a computer professional treats the same picture simply as a combination of pixels and colors. This technician is interested only in the diverse parameters that create the picture. Computer people understand that the computer picture is merely the superficial appearance of a particular combination of these forces. They know which elements need mending to yield a clearer, brighter, and sharper picture, and this is what they focus on.

In much the same way, every object and system in reality, including humankind and human society, reflects its unique, inherent combination of forces. To cope with any particular problem that arises, one must begin by understanding matter-behavior at its various levels. And for this to happen, we must reach deeper into the inherent force that designs and shapes matter.

The inherent force within each matter and object is generally referred to as "the will to exist." This force designs the shape of the substance and defines its qualities and comportment.

There are infinite forms and combinations of the will to exist, which is at the basis of all the substance in the world. A higher degree of substance reflects a greater desire to exist, and the differing desires in each of the degrees of substance—the still, vegetative, animate, and the speaking (human)—shape the various processes unfolding within it.

The desire to exist follows two principles: 1) keeping its present shape, meaning continuing to exist; and 2) adding to itself anything it senses is necessary for its existence. The desire to add something to itself is what distinguishes between the various degrees of matter. Let us look at this a bit more closely.

At the still level is the smallest desire to exist. This is because the wants of the still are small and it does not need to add anything exterior to itself in order to exist. Its only wish is to preserve its present shape, its structure, and its qualities. Additionally, it rejects anything alien. Because its only wish is to *not* change, it is called "still."

At the vegetative level, there is a stronger desire to exist. It is fundamentally different from the still's desire in that the vegetative changes and the still does not.

The vegetative doesn't "settle" for preserving its existence, like the still, but undergoes certain processes.

Thus, the vegetative attitude toward the environment is active. For example, plants move toward the sun, and send their roots to sources of moisture. The vegetative is dependent upon the environment—the sun, the rain, temperature, moisture, and drought—for its existence. The vegetative receives its necessities for sustenance from the environment, decomposes them, and constructs from them everything it needs. Then it secretes what is harmful to it and grows. Thus, the vegetative form is much more dependent on its environment than the still.

The vegetative has its own life cycle—plants live and die. Nevertheless, plants of the same kind grow, blossom and droop by the same rules. In other words, all the plants of a certain kind operate in the same way, and specific elements in the species do not have singularity of their own.

The greater a form's will to exist, the more it depends on the environment and its sensitivity to it. This connection becomes clearer at the animate degree, where the will to exist is greater than in the vegetative. For the most part, animals live in groups, packs. They are very mobile and must constantly roam in search of food and suitable living conditions. Animals eat other animals or other plants, and relate to them as a source of energy for their sustenance.

The animate degree manifests a certain level of development of personality, which prompts individual sensations and emotions, and lends a unique character to each animal. Every animal senses its environment on a personal level, brings itself closer to the beneficial, and moves farther away from the detrimental.

The life cycle of animals is also individual. Each lives and dies in its own time, unlike plants, whose life cycle is dictated by the season in the year.

The greatest degree of the will to exist is the human degree. Man is the only creature completely dependent upon others, and only man senses the past, present, and future. Humans affect the environment, and the environment affects them. Consequently, we human beings change ceaselessly, and not only because we are happy or unhappy in our present state, but because of our awareness of others, which makes us want everything others have.

Moreover, we want to have *more* than others have, or that others will not have, thus improving our state relative to others, as well as our sensation of self-gratification. This is why, in man, the will to exist is called "ego," "desire to enjoy," or "will to receive delight and pleasure," which Kabbalists refer to as the "will to receive."

Rabbi Yehuda Ashlag, known as Baal HaSulam,[8] says about that: "The will to receive is all the substance of Creation, from beginning to its end. Thus, all the numerous creations, their multitude incidents, and the ways by which they are conducted, that have appeared and that will appear are only measures and changes in the values of the will to receive."[9]

Humans are not only a slightly more evolved living creature; they are fundamentally different from the animate degree. At birth, a human being is a helpless being. But as we grow, we rise above all other creations. A newly born calf and a mature bull are distinguished primarily by their sizes, not by their wisdom. A human infant, however, is practically powerless and totally helpless. But gradually, over many years, it grows and evolves.

Hence, a young animal's development is very different from that of a human toddler. Our sages put it this way: "A day-old calf is called an ox."[10] It means that as soon as a calf is born, it is considered an ox because hardly any substantial qualities are added to it as it grows.

Humans, unlike all other creatures, need many years to evolve. When a baby is born, it hardly wants anything. But as it grows, its will to receive intensifies and evolves tremendously. When a new desire surfaces, it produces new needs, which the human being feels compelled to satisfy. To satisfy the new needs successfully, the brain evolves, as we begin to contemplate ways to satisfy the new desire. It follows that the brain's intellectual and conceptual evolution is a consequence of the intensification of our desire to enjoy.

We can observe how this principle works by examining how we bring up our children. To help them grow, we create challenging games for them, and their desire to succeed in the game makes them contemplate new ways of coping, which facilitates their progress. From time to time we make the game more difficult to help them evolve and continue their progress. Hence, unless one feels that something is missing, one will never be able to evolve. It is only when we want something that we begin to activate our intellects and ponder how we can obtain our desires.

The fact that a human being is comprised of both intellect and emotion enhances our will to receive, as the mind and the heart complement each other and increase our ability to perceive things that can induce pleasure. For this reason, our willpower is not limited by time or place. For example, we cannot feel events that happened a thousand years ago, but we can (and do) understand past events, which compensates for our inability to sense them. Thus, through our intellect we can bring ourselves to the point that we can actually experience them.

The opposite is also possible: if we sense something and want to examine how this might affect us, positively or negatively, we can analyze the situation with our intellect and join it to our sensation of the object. Thus, the mind and the heart expand our perception of time and place until we become unlimited. Therefore, a person living in a certain time or place might want to act like someone he or she had heard of, even if there was a great distance from the object of such admiration, either in time or distance. This is why people sometimes want to be like great historic figures.

When our will to receive is satisfied, we experience it as pleasure. When we cannot satisfy our desires we feel empty, frustrated, and even begin to suffer. Because of that, our happiness depends on the presence or absence of fulfillment of our desires. Any act we may perform, from the simplest to the most complex, is done to achieve but one thing—intensification of pleasure or diminution of pain. In fact, these are two sides of the same coin.

In his essay, "The Peace," Baal HaSulam states, "It is well known to researchers of nature that one cannot perform even the slightest movement without motivation, meaning without somehow benefiting oneself. When, for example, one moves one's hand from the chair to the table it is because one thinks that by putting one's hand on the table one will thus receive greater pleasure. If one would not think so, one would leave one's hand on the chair for the rest of one's life without moving it an inch, and all the more so with great efforts."

Man's uniqueness, compared to the rest of Nature, is not only in the power and quality of his desires. It is also in the fact that man's desires constantly increase and change, both during the lifetime of an individual, and throughout the generations. Examining the evolutionary history of other species, such as primates, indicates that several thousand years ago, primates were practically identical to those living today. While it is true that primates, too, change, as does any element in Nature, these are biological changes, like the geological changes occurring in minerals. Humankind, however, has gone through substantial changes over time.

EVOLUTION
OF THE HUMAN DESIRE FOR PLEASURE

The evolution of the desire for pleasure caused man to sense a constant need to develop, to invent, and to discover new things. A greater desire means greater needs, which yield keener intellectual and perception abilities. The growth of the will to receive generated humanity's evolution in the following ways:

First, the will to enjoy manifested in physical desires, such as the desire for sustenance, reproduction, and family. These desires have existed since the dawn of humanity. But because man is a social being, additional desires evolved within us, called "human desires" or "social desires," such as the desire for wealth, honor, sovereignty, and fame. These desires changed the face of humanity, introducing social classes, hierarchical systems, and changes in the socioeconomic structures.

Subsequently, there came the desire to enjoy knowledge. This desires manifested in the evolution of science, education systems, and culture. Its traces first appeared during the Renaissance and continued through the Industrial and Scientific Revolutions, and into the present day.

The growth of the Enlightenment Movement and the secularism of society were further manifestations of the desire for knowledge. This desire required that man understand all about his surrounding reality. Therefore, he sought more and more information, and wanted to research and control everything.

If we observe human evolution in culture, education, science, and technology in light of the understanding that desires lead all these processes, we will conclude that evolving desires also created all our ideas, inventions, and innovations. All of them are merely "technical" tools, "servants" that have evolved to fulfill the needs that these desires created.

This process of desire-evolution happens not only in the whole of humanity throughout history; it happens in the private lives of each of us as well. These desires surface in us one-by-one in a variety of combinations, and direct the course of our lives.

In fact, the internal engine that propels us forward and induces the processes that unfold in human society is actually our *desire to enjoy*. The evolution of our desires is ceaseless, and designs both our present and our future.

2

THE BOUNDARIES OF JOY

> In this world there are only two tragedies.
> One is not getting what one wants, and
> the other is getting it. The last is much
> the worst; the last is a real tragedy!
>
> ~Oscar Wilde, *Lady Windermere's Fan*

If we examine the pleasure we derive from having knowledge, domination, honor, wealth, or pleasure from food or sex, it seems that in all these cases, the greatest pleasure is experienced in the brief encounter between the desire and its satisfaction. From the moment we begin to fulfill our desires, the pleasure diminishes.

Pleasure from satisfying a desire may last minutes, hours or days, but it does fade. Even if we spend many years trying to obtain something, like a prestigious office, once we have it, we lose the sensation of pleasure.

Apparently, the pleasure that satisfied the desire is also what ended it.

Moreover, when pleasure permeates desire, and subsequently departs, this builds within us a desire to enjoy that is twice as strong as the original desire. What satisfies us today will not satisfy us tomorrow. We want more, much more. Thus, satisfying our desires eventually increases them and compels us to make even greater efforts to satisfy them.

When the desire to obtain things diminishes, one's sensation of life and one's vitality diminish. This is how human society constantly provides each member new desires, which revive us for another fleeting moment. However, time and time again we are filled for a moment and then drained once more, only to become more frustrated.

Today's society impels us to acquire more and more, to purchase almost everything, even when we do not have the means. Aggressive marketing, the need to meet social standards, and the ease of getting credit lead us to purchase far above our incomes.

Yet, once we have purchased something new, the excitement of possessing the new item soon fades as though it was never there, although the payments stay with us for years. In these cases, the disappointment from the purchase is not forgotten over time, but rather accumulates.

Wealth, too, does not bring happiness. New research, headed by Prof. Daniel Kahneman,[11] reveals that there is a huge gap between the "ordinary person's" assessment of the effect of parameters such as wealth and physical state on one's mood, and their actual impact according to the measurements made in the research. The research measured people's day-to-day mood and found no significant difference between rich and poor.

Moreover, negative moods (anger and hostility) were more frequent among the rich. One of the explanations for the absence of a stronger link between wealth and day-to-day happiness is that we quickly become accustomed to comfort and our new standard of living, and immediately want more.

We can summarize the boundaries of the desire to enjoy in the words of Baal HaSulam: "This world is created with a want and emptiness of the good abundance. And in order to acquire possessions, movement is required. However, it is known that profusion of movement pains humans... However, it is also impossible to remain devoid of possessions and good... Consequently, we choose the torment of movement to acquire the possessions. However, because all their possessions are for themselves alone, and 'he who has a single portion wants a double portion,' one finally dies with only 'half one's desire in one's hand.' In the end, they suffer from both sides—from the increase of pain due to the multiplicity of movement, and from the regret at not having the possessions they need to fill their empty half."[12]

It follows that the desire to enjoy places us in an evidently impossible situation. On the one hand, our desires constantly grow. On the other hand, fulfilling them, which costs us so heavily in effort and action, yields very short-lived satisfaction, which leaves us twice as empty.

FOOLING THE DESIRE TO ENJOY

As time went by, humanity developed various methods to cope with its inability to satisfy the desire to enjoy. For the most part, these methods were based upon two principles, which actually "fool" the desire to enjoy: 1) acquiring satisfying habits, and 2) diminishing the desire to enjoy.

The first principle relies on acquiring habits through conditioning. First, a child is taught that a certain act yields rewards. Once the required act is performed, the child is awarded by receiving the appreciation of teachers and the social environment. As the child grows, the reward is gradually stopped, but by now this act is "registered" in the adult's mind as rewarding.

Once an individual is accustomed to performing certain acts, the actual performance becomes satisfying. Thus, one becomes meticulous in the performance and feels great satisfaction when he or she improves it. Additionally, this *modus operandi* is usually accompanied by promises of future, sometimes even postmortem, rewards.

The second principle is based upon diminishing the desire to enjoy. It is much sadder to want and not to have, than to not want at all. The former suffers, while the latter is "content" to settle for what's available. Eastern teachings took these methods to the extreme and developed a wide variety of ways to decrease the intensity of the desire to enjoy. They used mental and physical exercises to do so, thus decreasing the intensity of the suffering.

As long as we remain preoccupied with chasing the next pleasure, we maintain our daily routines and hope for the best. While we may feel deficient and dissatisfied for not having what we want, the mere chase of the desired pleasure often serves as an acceptable substitute for the actual fulfilling of the desire. The chase makes us feel alive because we find ourselves continuously pursuing new goals and new desires, hoping to be satisfied by accomplishing them, or at least by working to attain them.

Thus far, it seems, we have wisely utilized these methods. But as the desire to enjoy grows, these solutions seem less and less effective. The growing egoism of humankind no longer allows us to subjugate ourselves to bogus resolutions or to silence it. This is apparent in every realm of life, from the very personal level to the level of the whole of humanity.

One such example that demonstrates the intensification of the ego is the decline of the family institution. Family relationships in general, and particularly between husband and wife, are the first to be hit by intensifying egoism, since our spouses are usually the closest people to us. The growing ego makes it difficult for us to belong to one another and to our families.

Previously, the family institution was shielded from upheaval; it was an island of stability. When there were problems in the world, we went out and fought. If we had troubles with our neighbors, we could always move. But the family unit was always a safe haven.

Even when we didn't really want to stay in the family, we would do it because of the children or because of the parents who needed our care. But today, the ego has become so overblown that we take nothing into consideration. The proliferation of divorce and single-parent families testify to this fact, despite the great difficulties they pose for the children. The recent increase in the number of old-age homes, an unheard of institution in the past, is yet another testimony to the disintegration of families.

The intensification of the ego has global effects, too. These consequences are far-reaching and place us in an unprecedented situation: on the one hand, globalization shows us how connected we all are—in economy, culture, science, education, and every other realm. On the other hand, our egos have evolved to the point that we cannot stand other people.

In truth, we have always been individual parts of a single system. But until today, we were unaware of it. Nature reveals it in the way that two forces act in sync: there is a connecting force that connects us all as one, and a rejecting force that pushes us away from one another. Thus, when these two forces begin to manifest their orientations more acutely, we begin to discover how dependent we are, and at the same time, we revolt against this dependency because of our growing egos. If we do not end our growing intolerance, alienation, and animosity, we will ultimately destroy one another.

Baal HaSulam warned about this danger long ago. Before he died, he explained that if we did not take a sharp turn away from the egoistic path, we would find ourselves engaged in a third and even a fourth world war. He warned that these would be nuclear wars that would result in the obliteration of most of the world's population.

Albert Einstein expressed a similar fear in a 24 May, 1946 telegram: "The unleashed power of the atom has changed everything, save our modes of thinking, and we thus drift toward unparalleled catastrophe." Regrettably, today their words seem more pertinent than ever.

Throughout history, we believed that better times were ahead, that we would progress in science, technology, culture, and education, all of which would make our lives better and happier. One of the places that best demonstrates that belief is Spaceship Earth, an attraction at Disney World's Epcot Center in Orlando, built in the beginning of the 1980s. Here, visitors are led through stops at historic landmarks in the evolution of humanity.

The journey begins with prehistoric cave paintings and continues through all the landmarks of human evolution, such as the beginning of the use of paper and wood. It ends with man's conquest of space. The attraction is designed according to the predominant approach of its time, and is therefore constructed as an ode to man. Human history is presented as a continuous march toward bliss, with an attitude of "It'll be here tomorrow, and if not tomorrow then the day after tomorrow; if not for our children, then for our grandchildren."

Now, a few years later, this optimistic approach is no longer valid. Each of us has everything one could only dream of a hundred years ago: infinite options for recreation, travel, rest, sports—the list is endless, yet we no longer believe in a better future. The formerly rosy picture has turned into a looming darkness, indicated by escalating suicide rates, violence, terror, eco-tragedies, social, economic, and political instability.

We are at a crossroads. We are beginning to sober up and see that a bright future is not a given. Instead, it seems far more likely that our children will not have lives as good as ours. The sense of comprehensive crisis at both individual and collective levels comes from our awareness that everything we have developed has failed to produce lasting happiness.

This is also the root of sensations such as meaninglessness and emptiness; hence, depression and drugs are the bane of our days. These are expressions of the helplessness that we feel because we don't know how to satisfy our desires to enjoy. Our egos have now grown to a point where nothing familiar satisfies them.

A typical demonstration of the hopelessness we feel is youth's attitude to life. Many young people treat life very differently than their parents did when they were the same age. There is a whole wide world before them, with numerous opportunities for success and self-realization. Yet, more and more young people lose interest in these objectives. It seems that young people have no interest in realizing their great potential. They seem to know in advance that at the end of the day, it will be pointless.

They also see the adults around them, who have attempted so much but are still not happy. Seeing this hardly adds to their desire to work! It is difficult for parents to understand why this is so, because when they were young, they were so different. However, it is so because each generation carries with it the experiences, and the disenchantments, of previous generations.

From here on, no known solution will help us improve our situation. We will be able to see where we are erring only if we learn the basis of Nature, by which every living organism exists, as well as the whole of Nature. To have a meaningful, secure, and peaceful life, we must know the perfect method to satisfy the desire to enjoy, the ego.

3

ALTRUISM IS LIFE'S LAW

When we research Nature, we discover the phenomenon of altruism. The word, "altruism," comes from the Latin word, *alter*, which means "other." The 19th century French philosopher, Auguste Comte, defined altruism as "the opposite of egoism." Other common definitions of altruism are "love of others," "devotion of self to love of others," "excessive generosity," "a predilection to work for the good of others," and "non-egoistic care for others."

Like egoism, altruism is a term that fits no other creature besides man. This is because concepts such as "intention" and "free will" relate only to the human species. Other creatures have no freedom of choice. Acts of giving and receiving, intake and emission, as well as prowling and self-sacrifice are rooted in other animals' genetic codes.[13] However, we will "borrow" these terms and use them with respect to animals so we can explain the laws of Nature more easily, and draw conclusions for humans.

At first glance, Nature seemed like a ring of egoists where only the fittest survive. This led researchers to cultivate various theories explaining the direct or indirect motives of animals to act altruistically.[14] However, more intense scrutiny and a broader perspective reveal that every struggle and confrontation actually increases the balance in Nature, and the reciprocal support of sustenance. These struggles yield better health and an overall improved evolution of Nature's creatures.

Another example of the balance in Nature can be found in the early 1990s, when the North Korean government decided to get rid of street cats that had become a nuisance. Several weeks after the eradication of most of the cats, there was a major increase in the number of mice, rats, and snakes. In fact, the North Korean government had to import cats from neighboring countries to correct this imbalance.

Wolves are another classic example. We are accustomed to treating wolves as ruthless and dangerous animals. However, when the wolves' population diminished, their contribution to balancing the deer, wild boar, and rodent populations became evident. As it turned out, unlike people, who prefer to hunt the healthy animals, wolves hunt primarily the sick and the weak, and in so doing contribute to the health of the animals in the area.

Thus, the more scientific research progresses, the more it reveals that all parts of Nature are interconnected parts of a single, comprehensive system. Indeed, when we project our own emotions on natural phenomena, we often feel that Nature can be cruel. But in truth, the eating of one creature by another guarantees the harmony and health of the collective system. In fact, in our own bodies, billions of cells die each minute and billions others are born. This is precisely what the continuation of life depends on!

HARMONY AMONG CELLS IN A LIVING ORGANISM

Within each multi-cellular organism is an intriguing phenomenon. If we examine each cell as a separate unit, we will see that it functions egoistically, thinking only of itself. However, when we examine it as a part of a system, the cell seems to take only the minimum required for its own sustenance, aiming the bulk of its activity toward the body. It behaves like an altruist, "thinks" only of the body's wellbeing, and acts accordingly.

There must be complete harmony among all the cells in a body. The nucleus of each cell contains the genetic code that encompasses all the body's information. Theoretically, this is all the information needed to recreate the whole body.

Each cell in the body must be aware of the whole body. It must know what the body needs and what it can do for it. Were this not so, the body would not persist. A cell in a body exists in a state of "consideration" for the body as a whole. All the cell's actions, the beginning and

the end of its division, specification of cells, and movement toward a certain location in the body, unfold in
congruence with the body's needs.

CONNECTEDNESS
CREATES LIFE IN A NEW DEGREE

Even though all the cells in our bodies contain identical genetic information, each cell puts a different part
of that information into action, depending on its place
and functionality in the body. When the embryo is just
beginning to evolve, all its cells are identical. But as the
embryo evolves, the cells differentiate, and each cell acquires qualities of a specific kind.

Thus, each cell has its own "mind" or "awareness,"
but the altruistic connectedness among cells enables
them to create a new being, a complete body whose mind
and awareness belong to a higher degree and are not present within this or that cell, but rather in the bonding
between them.

AN EGOISTIC CELL IS A CANCEROUS CELL

Healthy cells are restricted by a wide variety of rules and
limitations. However, cancerous cells have no regard at
all for restrictions. Cancer is a state where the body is
consumed by its own cells, which have embarked on un-
inhibited proliferation. While multiplying, a cancer cell
divides relentlessly, regardless of the needs of its environment and irresponsive to the body's commands.

Cancer cells destroy their environment, thus creating open spaces for them to grow. They impel the neighboring blood vessels to grow into the resulting tumor to nourish it, and thus subjugate the whole body to themselves.

In simple terms, cancer cells induce the death of the body through acts of egoism. They operate in this manner even though it does not bring them any benefit. Actually, the truth is to the contrary, as the death of the body means the death of its assassins, too. The manner in which cancerous cells take over the host body leads them to their own demise. Thus, when egoism nurtures itself, it leads everything to death, including itself. Egoistic behavior and general inattentiveness to the needs of the whole body lead them straight to doom.

THE INDIVIDUAL VS. THE COLLECTIVE

In a healthy body, cells "relinquish" their own lives in favor of that of the body, when necessary. When genetic errors occur in cells, which may turn them into cancerous cells, the cell activates a mechanism that ends its life. The fear that it might become cancerous and jeopardize the entire body makes the cell give up its own life for the life of the body.

We can find a similar altruistic action, though under different circumstances, in the way the cellular slime mold (*Dictyostelium mucoroides*) lives. Under ideal conditions, the mold lives in the form of separate cells that provide for their own food and multiply independently. But when there is shortage of food, the cells unite and create a multi-cellular body. While building this body, some of the cells give up their own lives to promote the survival of the other cells.

HELPING OTHERS

The primate researcher, Frans de Waal, introduces many more examples of altruism in Nature in his book, *Good Natured.*[15] In one of the experiments he describes, two primates were separated from each other by a transparent partition that allowed them to see one another. Each of them was given food at different times, and the monkeys tried to hand over the food across the see-through partition.

Observations revealed that the monkeys tended to increase their alertness and care for another when one of them was hurt or handicapped. A crippled female monkey managed to survive for two decades in a rough climate, and even raise five offspring, thanks to the assistance given to her by the other monkeys.

Another female monkey, mentally and physically retarded, survived with the support of her older sister, who dragged her on her back for a very long time and protected her. A female monkey that had lost her sight was granted special guard by the males. A male baboon whose brother had an epileptic episode stood beside his ailing brother, rested his hand on his brother's chest and firmly prevented the caretakers who wanted to examine him from approaching.

Other animals act very similarly. Dolphins support their wounded companions and keep them close to the water level to keep them from drowning. Elephants have joined to help one of their own that was dying on the sand. They tried their hardest to pick him up by pushing their trunks and their tusks under his body. Some even broke their tusks in the process. Lastly, friends of a female elephant that had been hit by a poacher's bullet to her lungs, bent under her to prevent her from falling.

A COMMUNAL SOCIETY AMONG ANIMALS

The animal world presents some spectacular examples of communal societies where each element works to benefit the whole. Such societies include ants, mammals, and birds.

Biologists Avishag and Amotz Zahavi researched the communal life of the Arabian Babbler, a songbird found in large numbers in the arid lands of the Middle East. They described many altruistic phenomena. The Arabian Babblers live in groups, co-operate in defending their territory, and collectively tend to the single nest within it. While the other birds are eating, one remains to guard the group despite its own hunger. Babblers that find food offer it to their friends before they themselves are full. They feed the young of the other members in the group and tend to their every need. When a predator approaches, the Babblers squeak in alarm to warn their group members, even at the risk of exposing themselves to danger. They also risk themselves to save a member that's been captured by a predator.

INTERDEPENDENCY

Scientific research has found numerous examples of interdependency. One such example is the yucca plant, which has a symbiotic (interdependent) relationship with the yucca butterfly. The female butterfly helps fertilize the flower by transmitting powder from the stamens of one flower and placing them precisely on the style of another flower. Subsequently, the female butterfly lays her eggs in the place where the flower seeds will develop. When the larva hatch, they feed off the growing buds of the yucca plant. However, they leave enough buds on the plant to allow the continuation of the plant. By sustaining this kind of relationship, both plant and butterfly ensure the continuation of their species.

WITHOUT POVERTY OR LACK

In an essay written in 2002, Prof. Theodore C. Bergstrom explains that in a human-free environment, animals live by what is beneficial to the environment, not by the law of "survival of the fittest," as is usually believed.[16] In such a society, animals maintain a balanced existence, and the population density is always adapted to current living conditions. There is never any shortage or deprivation in any part of the population unless there is an "accident," which the animal society corrects as quickly as possible. Society persists in a manner that places each of its elements in the ideal conditions for survival and for optimal use of the environment's resources.

IN NATURE,
EVERYTHING MOVES TOWARD UNITY

Nature's evolution proves that the process of turning the world into a global village is not coincidental. Rather, it is a natural stage, as civilization evolves toward comprehensive harmony.

According to evolutionary biologist Elisabet Sahtouris, at the end of the process there will be one system whose parts will be interconnected in reciprocity and collaboration. In a lecture given at a conference in Tokyo in 2005, Sahtouris explained that evolution is comprised of phases of individualization, conflict, and competition. At the end of these stages the elements unite into a single, harmonious system.

She used as an example the evolutionary process of life on Earth. Billions of years ago, Earth was inhabited by bacteria. The bacteria proliferated and thus began to compete for Nature's resources, such as food and territories. Consequently, a new entity—a bacterial colony—was formed, which was better suited to the environmental conditions.

A bacteria is actually a community of bacteria that functions as a single organism. By these very rules, unicellular creatures began to evolve and became multicellular creatures, ultimately comprising complex bodies of plants, animals, and people.

Each distinct element has a personal, egoistic interest. However, the essence of evolution is that elements with personal interest unite into a single body and work for the collective interest of that body. Sahtouris regards the process that humanity is presently undergoing as a necessary step to forming a single human family—a community that will provide for the interest of us all, provided we function as healthy parts within it.

Thus, if we thoroughly examine Nature's elements, we will see that altruism is the basis for life. Every living organism and every system consist of an assemblage of cells or parts that cooperate, complement one another, and help one another. They share and survive by the altruistic law, "One for all." As we look deeper into Nature, we will find more and more examples of Nature's reciprocal connectedness, and that Nature's general law is "altruistic bonding among egoistic elements."

Nature designed life in such a way that each cell must become altruistic toward others in order to build a living body. Nature created a regularity by which the adhesive that joins the cells and the organs as a living body is the altruistic relationship among them. Thus, it follows that the force that creates and sustains life is altruistic, a force of giving and sharing. Its objective is to create a life based on altruistic existence, harmonious, and balanced among all its elements.

4

BREACHING THE BALANCE

> *O Man! Seek no further for the*
> *author of evil; thou art he.*
>
> ~Jean-Jacques Rousseau, *The Creed of a Savoyard Priest*

> *For man is the cruelest animal.*
>
> ~Friedrich Nietzsche, *Thus Spake Zarathustra*

> *Man is the Only Animal that*
> *Blushes. Or needs to.*
>
> ~Mark Twain, *Following the Equator*

Except for the human ego, all of Nature's elements operate according to the law of altruism. They are in balance with their environments and create harmonious systems. When the balance is breached, the organism begins to disintegrate. Thus, the ability to reconstruct the balance is a necessary condition for the existence of life.

In fact, the body expends its entire protective power on maintaining the balance. When we speak of a strong body or a weak body, we refer to its ability to preserve its balance. Preserving the balance requires each element to act altruistically regarding the system it is part of, and which provides the basis of Nature's comprehensive harmony and perfection. If a certain element does not abide by life's principle of altruism, it thus breaches the balance. These two terms—altruism and balance—are therefore intertwined by way of cause and effect.

In all creatures but man, there is a "balancing software" that makes them perform whatever is required to maintain balance at any given moment. Other creatures always know what to do, and hence do not stumble upon uncertainties or unfamiliar situations where they are unaware of how to behave within the new environment. They are not free to act at will, and are therefore clearly unable to change Nature's balance. Human Beings are the only creatures in whom this balancing software is *not* installed.

Because Nature does not instill in us sufficient knowledge or instincts to exist in balance with Nature from birth, we are uncertain of how to behave correctly in human society, i.e. how to be in balance with the people around us. The balanced state is also the happiest—a perfect state where everything runs harmoniously, without the need to create resistance or erect protective walls.

The absence of a balancing software takes our social evolution in an egoistic direction, and this has intensified with each passing generation. In consequence, the way man tries to satisfy his desire to enjoy does not take others' existence into consideration. We do not aspire to bond with others altruistically, as is done in Nature, and consequently, we do not know that it is in so doing that we will find the perfect joy we so crave.

If we look within, we will find that we truly consider only our own existence. All of our relationships with others are simply aimed at improving our own state. To improve our lives by even the slightest bit, we agree to see those for whom we have no need disappear completely.

No other creature but man can plunder its surroundings. No other creature can derive satisfaction by oppressing others, drawing pleasure from their suffering. Only man can experience satisfaction at another's sorrow. There is a well-known maxim that states that it is much safer to walk next to a satiated lion than next to a satiated human being.

The egoistic goals that have grown in us from generation to generation, often at the expense of others, are in sharp contrast to Nature's fundamental aim: to give each and every element an optimal existence. This is why human egoism is the only detrimental force in the world, the only force that tips the balance in Nature's overall system.

In his essay, "Peace in the World," Baal HaSulam writes, "The equal side in all the people of the world is that each and every one of us stands ready to abuse and exploit all the people for his own private benefit with every means possible, and without taking into consideration that he is going to build himself on the ruin of his friend." And he adds further: "man ...feels that all the people in the world should be under his own government and for his own private use. And this is a law that cannot be breached. And the only difference is in the choices of people. One chooses to exploit people by attaining the lower desires, and one by attaining government, while a third by attaining respect. Furthermore, if one could do it without much effort, he would agree to exploit the whole world with all three together: wealth, government, and respect. However, he is forced to choose according to his ability and capability."

It is interesting to see that to pave the way to a peaceful life we must first thoroughly understand our egoistic nature. In fact, says Baal HaSulam, it is no coincidence, and it is irreproachable, that our egoism is intensifying. It is happening to show us precisely how far off we are from the general law of reality, the law of altruism, which is at the basis of our lives, and to induce us to correct this distance.

The purpose of the intensification of the ego is to make us acknowledge the opposite orientation of our egos, which want only to receive for themselves at others' expense, from Nature's comprehensive force, whose quality is altruism, love, and sharing. From here on, we will relate to our oppositeness from Nature's force as "imbalance with Nature," or simply, "imbalance," and to acquiring the quality of altruism as "balance with Nature."

WHAT GIVES US PLEASURE?

As we have said above, our desires are divided into physical-existential desires, and human-social desires. We will now focus on the human-social desires to understand what causes imbalance in our relationships with others.

Human-social desires are divided into three primary categories: desires for wealth, desires for honor and sovereignty, and desires for knowledge. These categories symbolize all the non-physical desires that can surface within us. They received the name "human-social desires" for two reasons: a) These are desires that one "absorbs" from society. If we lived alone, we would not want these things. b) These desires can be realized only within a society.

To be precise, we should say that what is required for existence is called "physical," and anything beyond it is called "human-social." We can monitor how we use each desire for something that goes beyond what is necessary for sustenance. And actually, this is why such desires evolve in us.

Within each of us is a different blend of human-social desires, and this blend changes during our lives. One may have a greater desire for wealth, another for honor, and a third for knowledge. Each of these represents a different kind, or level, of desire.

- **Wealth** symbolizes one's desire to possess, to own. It is a desire to acquire the whole world so that it will become one's own.

- **Honor** is a higher level of desire. One no longer wants to "grab" everything like a child, but realizes that there is a wide world outside oneself, and is willing to work one's entire life to earn outsiders' respect. Such a person is even willing to pay for respect.

  The desire for money is more primitive than the desire for honor; it is a desire to snatch everything and attach it to oneself. A desire for honor, however, has no interest in annulling the other. One instead seeks authority, superiority over others, and their respect. Thus, honor represents man's desire to purchase the world as something that remains outside of it and respects it.

- **Knowledge** and the desire for it represent a greater desire for sovereignty. It is a desire to acquire knowledge, to know every detail in reality, to understand how everything unfolds, and how Nature and people can be manipulated to one's own benefit. This desire symbolizes man's desire to control and dominate everything through the mind.

Each desire beyond the basic desires to persist comes to us from our society. Success or failure in satisfying these desires is measured only with respect to our society. The previously mentioned research conducted by Prof. Kahneman, revealed that when people are asked to quantify the level of happiness they are feeling, they assess primarily by social standards.

The research also showed that our happiness stems less from what we have, and more from comparing our situations to those of our neighbors. This is also the reason that the level of happiness is not increasing as we become richer. As we earn more, we compare ourselves to richer and richer societies.

Thus, the only way we can determine our happiness or unhappiness is by comparing ourselves to others. When another person succeeds, we become envious. Deep within, and sometimes even overtly, we wish for the other person's failure. It is an uncontrollable, automatic reaction. When others fail, we are happy because it immediately improves our relative position.

In fact, human pleasures beyond the needs of the physical body depend on our attitude toward others, and on how we regard our relationships with others. It is not what we acquire that makes us feel good, but our superiority over others, the social esteem, and hence self-esteem, and the power to control that it grants us.

This egoistic attitude toward others creates imbalance and incongruity between us and the general law of Nature—the law of altruism. Our egoistic aspirations to rise above others, to enjoy at their expense, and to be separated from them contradicts Nature's pull to bring all its parts toward the point of altruistic bonding. Hence, egoism is the cause of all suffering.

There are laws in Nature that affect us even if we do not know them. This is because Nature's laws are absolute laws. If one breaks one of the laws, one's deflection from the rule operates on that person and compels him or her to obey the law once more.

We already know most of Nature's laws at the still, vegetative, and animate degrees, and in our own bodies, as well. However, in human relations, we are wrong to think that there are no laws. In fact, we cannot understand the laws of a certain degree while we are still within it. We only become aware of these laws when looking from a higher level. This is why we cannot make a clear connection between egoistic behavior toward others and negative phenomena in our lives.

CORRECT USE OF THE EGO

The fact that the ego creates imbalance in Nature does not mean that we need to revoke it. We only need to correct how we use it. Throughout history, humanity has tried numerous ways to annul the ego or artificially reduce it in order to reach equality, love, and social justice. Revolutions and social changes have come and gone, but all have failed because balance can only be acquired by correctly combining the full power of reception with the full power of bestowal.

In the previous chapter, we saw that the common law for all living organisms is the altruistic connection among egoistic elements. These two contradicting elements—altruism and egoism, giving and receiving—exist in every matter, creature, phenomenon, and process.

On the material level, the emotional level, or any other level, you will always find two forces, not just one. They complement and balance one another, and manifest in a variety of ways: as electrons and protons; a negative charge and a positive charge, rejection and attraction, acid and basic, and hate and love. Every element in Nature maintains a reciprocal relationship with the system supporting it, and these relationships consist of harmonious giving and receiving.

Nature aspires to bring us to perfection, to unlimited bliss. Hence, Nature has instilled in us a desire to enjoy. There is no need to cancel the ego; we need only correct it, or more accurately, change the way we use our desires to enjoy, moving from an egoistic approach to an altruistic one.

The correct evolution uses the full power of the desire to enjoy within us, but in its corrected form. Moreover, since the ego is our Nature, it is simply impossible to counteract it or restrain it indefinitely, because that would be going against Nature. If we try to do that, we will discover that we are unable to do so.

Although our present state does not indicate that Nature wishes for us to enjoy, it is because, unlike every other degree in Nature, our egos have not completed their development.

This is how Baal HaSulam explains it in his essay, "The Essence of Religion and Its Purpose": "From all of Nature's systems, presented before us, we understand that in any being of the four types—still, vegetative, animate, and speaking, both as a whole and in particular, we find a purposeful guidance, meaning a slow and gradual growth by way of cause and effect. This is similar to a fruit on a tree, guided to a favorable purpose of finally becoming a sweet and fine-looking fruit. And go and ask a botanist, how many phases the fruit undergoes from the time it becomes visible until it is completely ripe. Not only do its preceding phases show no evidence of its sweet and fine-looking end, but as if to vex, they show the opposite of the final shape: the sweeter the fruit is at its end, the more bitter it is in the earlier phases of its development."

The truth is, Nature's perfection is not apparent in any creature before it reaches its ultimate form. In the case of humans, our present state is not the complete and final state. This is why our state seems negative. However, just like the fruit on the tree, there is nothing within us that we need to ruin, or it wouldn't have been placed within us to begin with.

The ego's force is a wonderful thing. It brought us this far, and thanks to it, we will also reach our perfection. It is the ego that pushes us forward and facilitates unlimited progress. Without it, we would not have evolved as a human society, and we would not be fundamentally different from animals. Finally, thanks to our egos, we are now arriving at a situation where we are no longer willing to settle for ephemeral, familiar pleasures, but want to have what lies beyond them.

The trick is to find the best and wisest way to use our ego to progress toward altruistic bonding with others. And the method that enables us to do that is the wisdom of Kabbalah. This is also the origin of its name. *Kabbalah* means to receive. *Hence, the wisdom of Kabbalah is the wisdom of how to receive the perfect pleasure, in the perfect way.*

Kabbalah does not require that we suppress our natural egoistic drives. On the contrary, it acknowledges their existence and explains how we can best and most effectively use them to reach perfection.

During our evolution, we are required to combine all the inclinations and elements within us harmoniously, and harness them to the process. For instance, we normally think of envy, lust, and honor in negative terms. There is even a well-known maxim that says, "Envy, lust, and honor bring a man out of the world" (Avot, 4:21).

What is not so familiar, however, is the deeper meaning of this maxim. The world that envy, lust, and honor bring us from is this world; but the world they bring us *to* is the spiritual world, a higher degree of Nature. However, there is a condition: it happens only if we channel these natural inclinations in a positive and beneficial direction, enabling us to attain balance with Nature's altruistic force.

THE CRISIS
AS AN OPPORTUNITY
TO RESTORE BALANCE

The Chinese use two brush strokes to write the word 'crisis.' One brush stroke stands for danger; the other for opportunity. In a crisis, be aware of the danger, but recognize the opportunity.

-John F. Kennedy,
from a speech in Indianapolis, April 12, 1959

Nature aspires to balance. All its actions are aimed at bringing each part into balance. With volcanoes, for example, the pressures deep within Earth increase until Earth's crust cannot balance them. The resolution of this imbalance is a volcanic eruption, which balances the underground pressure with surface pressure. This is Nature's way of balancing an unbalanced state.

The laws of physics and chemistry explain that the only reason for any movement of matter or object is the quest for balance. To achieve this balance, such phenomena as equilibrium of pressures, concentrations, temperatures, the flowing of water to the lowest place, and the dispersal of heat and cold, are created. In scientific terms, a balanced state is called "homeostasis." (*Homo*, in Latin, means "same," and *stasis* means "state"). Homeostasis is the state to which everything in reality is attracted.

However, at the human level, homeostasis requires conscious participation. This is why, as long as we are not aware of the fact that an egoistic attitude toward others harms us and the world, we cannot be held accountable. Instead, Nature comes to our aid by showing us that there is an imbalance, which is why it is now leading us to a point of a comprehensive crisis in our egoistic evolution.

The purpose of the crisis is to make us realize that we are treading the wrong path and must change course. Thus, the crisis is not a punishment, but is intended to bring us to perfection.

As a matter of fact, there are no punishments in the world because it is not our fault that we are born egoists. All that exists in our world are means to develop us.

We must remember that human beings, who are essentially a desire to enjoy, cannot move an inch without a sensation of deficiency. In other words, we only move because of an absence of fulfillment of a desire, and hence we only move toward future fulfillment. When we lack something, when we are dissatisfied, we suffer and begin to look for solutions. This is how we progress and evolve.

The crisis is the emergence of the "faults" that have been deliberately instilled in us by Nature. These faults allow us to "correct" them by ourselves, and thus we elevate ourselves. In the past, hundreds and thousands of years ago, when humanity suffered, it couldn't understand why it was suffering. Now, we are ready to understand the reason, and to see that suffering points us straight toward acquiring the quality of altruism, Nature's quality of love and giving. This is why Nature can "ask" a contemporary person, "Are you responding correctly to what is being handed you?" Today, along with the pain, Nature admits us into the reason for it.

Until today, we have been treating Nature in a very straightforward manner: Nature prompted us to evolve by evoking desires within us, and we raced to evolve in numerous ways—through culture, education, science, and technology.

Today, however, we have suddenly reached an impasse, and we are forced to stop and examine ourselves. In fact, this is the moment when we receive the ability to examine our desires. Hence, from this moment on we are committed to continue with this examination. We cannot continue developing our awareness only of *how* to use our desires better; we must begin to think about our desires and review them from a new perspective. We have to start asking, "What am I doing with my desires, and for what?" Each of us is required to examine ourselves.

In fact, Nature's force is a constant altruistic force. It is unchanging and constantly pressures us to balance with it. The only thing that does change and grow, according to the embedded "program," is the ego within us. The ego's increasing contrast from Nature's force intensifies the imbalance, which we experience as pressure, discomfort, suffering, and other negative phenomena and crises.

The intensity of this pressure depends on the degree of our imbalance. This is why, in the past, suffering and discomfort were less, since egoism was smaller. Today, we find that it is increasing daily.

It follows that we alone determine the intensity of the suffering or happiness that we experience, depending on the level of our imbalance with Nature. In other words, the fact that we are non-integrated parts of an integrated system is the very cause of all suffering and the root of all adversities and crises.

When we tie all the manifestations of individual and collective crises with the human ego—the cause of the system's imbalance—we will be able to move toward a solution. When pain is accompanied by understanding its source, when the purpose of suffering is sensed, such pains are beneficial, since they have become the forces of progress.

Thus, the crisis is not a crisis, but a more progressive state of human evolution, which first appears as a negation of the present state. However, if we change our attitudes and our awareness, and view this from a different perspective, we will see that what now seems like a crisis is actually a golden opportunity.

5

Obeying Nature's Law

It is not possible to run a course aright when the goal itself has not been rightly placed.

~Francis Bacon

LIFE'S PURPOSE

The general force that operates and sustains Nature is an altruistic force. This force impels all parts of Nature to exist as organs in a single body, in balance, and in harmony. When these parts achieve this condition, they achieve the bonding called "life." This bonding exists at all degrees besides man; hence, it is the purpose of man's life to independently create this bonding. And this is exactly what Nature is goading us to achieve.

Such bonding is acquired through an altruistic attitude toward others, and is expressed in caring about others' well-being. This attitude grants perfect joy, since by creating this kind of bonding with others, one reaches equilibrium with Nature's comprehensive law and becomes completely integrated with Nature.

We are the only creatures that do not operate from a state of reciprocal bonding, and this is why we do not feel "life." Although it is true that we are "alive" in the superficial sense, in the future, we will discover that the term "life" actually relates to a completely different mode of existence.

The road that leads to the realization of life's purpose consists of a long phase of egoistic evolution, one that lasts several millennia. At the end of that period, we "sober up" from the notion that the ego will make us happy, and discover that the *increase* of egoism is at the basis of our every predicament!

Next, we must come to realize that we are each part of a single system. We need to begin to relate to others according to the law of altruism, and bond with them as compatible organs in a single body.

In the beginning, we will do this only to escape the problems in our lives, and our immediate reward will be relief from suffering on every realm in life. We will also be granted a new sense of meaning and substance in our lives. However, when we begin this process, we will discover that Nature's plans for us reach far beyond convenient living. If that were all there were to it, the balancing-software, the altruistic quality, would have been instilled in us just as it was instilled in animals.

But, in fact, we were created with an egoistic Nature only so we could understand by ourselves that the current form of our ego is harmful to us, since it is opposite from Nature's own quality. The independent search for balance gradually leads us to recognize the merits of altruism, the quality of loving and giving.

As we have seen, each element in Nature operates to benefit the system it is in. However, this balanced existence is instinctive, at the material level. The difference between man and the rest of the degrees in Nature is that man is a thinking being, and the power of thought is the most powerful force in reality.

The power of thought transcends all the inanimate forces, such as gravity, the electrostatic force, the magnetic force, and the forces of radiation. It is also above the force that prompts growth and evolution at the vegetative level, and above the force that prompts animals to be attracted to what benefits them, and repelled from what harms them. The power of thought is even above the force of man's egoistic desires.

Thus, while in the still, vegetative, and the animate, the good attitude of an element toward the system is expressed at the material level. With man, the level that requires correction is the level of thoughts and attitude toward others. *The Book of Zohar*, one of the seminal books in the wisdom of Kabbalah, written some 2,000 years ago by Rabbi Shimon Bar-Yochai, defines it thus: "All is clarified in the thought" (*The Zohar*, Part 2, item 254).[17]

Our inherent resistance to bond with other people into a single whole is an expression of our egoism. Altruism is the opposite; it is an intrinsic motion of a person, from within one's heart and one's desire, toward sensing others as part of oneself. Thus, to balance between us and Nature's law of altruism, we are required to be in a state where we want to enjoy our altruistic attitude to others, to enjoy bonding as parts of a single system, instead of wanting to exploit and dominate others.

The process of changing our source of pleasure from egoistic-based to altruistic-based is called *Tikkun* (correction) of the ego, or simply *Tikkun*. This process relies on the building of a new desire within us, a desire to acquire the attribute of altruism.

To progress in the correction process, we must use the power of thought. In his essay, "A Thought is an Upshot of the Desire," Baal HaSulam explains that our desire to enjoy determines what we will think about.

For example, he says that we do not think of things that contradict our desire, such as the day of our death. We only think of things that we want. And the desire begets the thought; it induces the appearance of thoughts that facilitate the realization of our desires.

However, continues Baal HaSulam, thought also has a special capability: it can act in the opposite direction. In other words, it can increase the desire. If we have a small desire for something, and we think about it, this desire will grow. And the more we think about it, the more the desire will grow.

This ability creates an intensifying cycle, where the growing desire intensifies the thought, and the thought continues to intensify the desire. Using this mechanism, we build a great desire for something we consider important, but for which we haven't the appropriate level of desire among our numerous desires. In this manner, we can make the desire to acquire the quality of altruism the center of our desires.

This brings up the question: "How can we increase our thoughts about altruistic bonding to others, when our desire for it is not the greatest desire within us? After all, at present, there are many more desires within us, and great desires, too, much more tangible and palpable, and they are the ones we think about." Or, more concisely, "How we can set this wheel of thought-desire-thought in motion?"

Here is where the influence of our social environment comes into play. If we know how to build around us the appropriate environment, it will serve as a source of new desires and thoughts, which will intensify our drive to attain Nature's quality of altruism. Because of the importance of man's social environment to his evolution, we will dedicate the next two chapters to this topic.

WHAT SHOULD WE DO?

We need to start thinking about the benefits of reaching equilibrium with Nature's force, recognizing that a positive future depends on that. We must focus our thoughts on being parts of a single, integrated system that contains all people wherever they are, and begin to relate to others accordingly.

A correct, altruistic attitude toward others means directing our intentions, thoughts, and concerns to the well-being of others. When our thoughts are aimed toward others, we wish everyone to receive all that they need for their sustenance. However, beyond physical well-being, we should focus our power of thought on elevating others' level of awareness. We must want every single person to feel part of the whole, and to function accordingly.

This is first and foremost an internal work, at the level of thought. It is important to contemplate this thought, and not let it out of our minds. We should ascribe such thoughts great importance, since our happiness and well-being depend on them. It is through them that we will be saved from our problems and adversities. At first, it may seem abstract, but a positive future depends precisely on that, and only on that.

Besides the internal altruistic attitude toward others—at the level of thought—we can also perform altruistic *actions* toward them: we can share our knowledge about the purpose of life and how to reach it. If we confer that knowledge on others and they become partners in the awareness of the problem, if they have the same thoughts and the same mindset concerning the solution, then we have prompted a positive change in the one system of which we are all part. As a result, our awareness will intensify even more, and we will immediately experience positive changes in our lives.

A single person who changes his or her attitude toward others induces change in the whole of humanity. In fact, we can picture the relationship between the individual and humanity in the following manner: You and all humankind are part of a single system. However, the other members of humanity are completely dependent upon the way you operate them. The whole world is in your hands. This is how reality is arranged for every single person.

To understand this, let us picture a cube with about seven billion layers, approximately the number of people on Earth. Each layer stands for one person and is operated by that person. Within each layer, there are seven billion cells, one of which is you. The rest of the cells symbolize the incorporation of the other people in you. This is how Nature's single system is built. In other words, every person is integrated into all the other people; hence, we are all tied to one another.

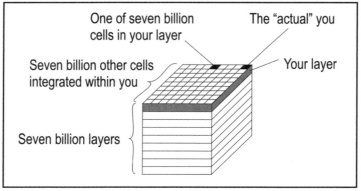

The integration of the individual
in Nature's single system

If you correct your attitude to even one of the other cells in your layer, you have awakened your own part in the other. This creates a positive change in that individual, which brings one closer to wanting to correct one's attitude toward others.

And that change affects more than just that one person. It affects that person's entire level, including all the other cells with which one is integrated. Moreover, each of the other cells has its own layer in the cube, and that layer, too, is now awakened.

In fact, when a single person corrects his or her attitude toward others, this instigates a chain of events, a process of unconscious, positive changes in the awareness of all people. Such interactions between layers in the cube promote all of humanity toward correction and wholeness.

We should keep in mind that at the moment, humanity is in contradiction to the altruistic Nature. Hence, even if we have made the slightest change at all, we have brought humankind just a little closer to balance with Nature. The increased balance means reduced imbalance, and along with it, reduction of negative phenomena.

Although people who have not corrected their attitude toward others will not feel it yet, those who induce this change will sense it immediately. Thus, the more we pursue these thoughts and actions to increase our awareness that we are parts of a single system, the sooner we will feel that we are living in a welcoming world, a joyful and good place.

Man's power of thought and his crucial impact on reality are expressed in the following words of the great Kabbalist, Rabbi Abraham Isaac HaCohen Kook (manuscript, p. 60): "It requires much accustoming to feel the power of life and the reality of the power of thought, to know the might of the concept and the enforcement of life, and strength of the reality of the thought. And by awareness, to understand that the more the thought ascends, refines, and polishes, man and the world ascend, refine, and polish. And all sides of reality, which are always below the power of thought, their ascents and descents depend on the ascent and descent of man's power of thought."

When one's thought rises, and he or she is rewarded by correcting one's attitude toward others, one acquires new aspirations:

- *Kesef* (money) comes from the word *Kisuf* (longing). This pertains to one's desire to acquire others' desires and care for their satisfaction, much like a mother tending to her children and enjoying providing for their needs.

- Respect—one respects every person and treats all as partners.

- Knowledge—one wishes to learn from every person so as to understand what others need, to bond with them and thus reach equilibrium with Nature. As a result, one is granted the understanding and the sensation of the altruistic thought that encircles reality: Nature's thought. This is the entrance to the highest degree in Nature, the perfection.

MUCH EASIER THAN IT SEEMS

The correction process, in which we change our source of pleasure from enjoying egoism to enjoying altruism, at first seems quite complicated. But reality is quite unlike its initial impression. In "Peace in the World," Baal HaSulam says: "At first glance, the plan seems imaginary, as something that is above human nature. But when we deeply delve into it, we will find that the contradiction from reception for oneself to bestowal upon others is nothing but a psychological matter."

The term "psychological matter" does not mean that it is a problem to be solved by therapists; rather, it indicates that the problem is with our internal attitude toward how we enjoy. We are used to deriving pleasure from egoistic fulfillments; it is hard for us to grasp that it is even possible to enjoy in some other way.

It seems easier to us to go along with the ego as it is without correcting it—to idle away and be carried by the streams of life, the "*que sera sera*" approach to life. But the truth is quite different. Although we are unaware of it, our ego, the one we so trust and rely on to always lead us to our optimum state, is not really "us." Rather, the ego is like a tyrant who sits within us and subjugates us to its demands. We have simply gotten used to thinking that these demands are our demands, and that our ego works to our benefit.

We need to recognize the ego as dominating us without asking if we are interested in that dominion, as tricking us and working within us as if *we* want certain things, when it is actually the ego that wants them. When we realize the amount of effort and energy it costs us to carry out the ego's demands of us, and the miniscule reward we receive for this tremendous effort, we will treat the ego, in its present, uncorrected form, as the worst of all tyrants.

Baal HaSulam says that if people compared the effort they make with the pleasure they actually experience in life, they would discover that "...the pain and suffering they endure to attain their sustenance is many times greater than the little pleasure they feel in this life" ("Introduction to The Study of the Ten Sefirot," item 3). However, this fact is hidden from us.

Our ego hides itself and clothes itself within us, as if we and it were the same. Time and time again, it impels us to aspire to egoistic pleasures. However, in truth, our essence is merely a desire to enjoy, not an egoistic desire to enjoy, as it may seem to us. In other words, "our" ego is not really our ego, and we should distinguish between the two.

In the moment one makes that distinction and wants to acquire the quality of altruism to balance with Nature, one immediately feels Nature's positive support. We should also note that there is a big difference between making an effort towards egoistic actions, and making an effort towards altruistic actions. Once an individual acquires Nature's quality, the altruistic actions one performs no longer require energy and effort. On the contrary, they are performed with ease and comfort, bringing sensations of elation, exhilaration, and satisfaction.

Actually, altruistic actions do not require energy; they produce it. The reason is that an altruistic force acts like the sun, which emits light and is a constant supplier of virtually unending energy. The egoistic force, however, always wants to receive and to acquire; hence, it is always in deficit.

One can compare this phenomenon to the positive and negative poles in an electric battery. The minute one identifies oneself with the positive force, one feels energized and filled with unending capabilities. One becomes like an endless spring that creates and releases infinite energy from within itself.

Hence, as Baal HaSulam said, the problem facing us is merely psychological—to become detached from egoistic calculations, which only seemingly benefit us, and switch to altruistic calculations. In this manner, we are guaranteed that our will to receive will experience immediate and unlimited pleasure, since real and complete pleasures are found in altruistic bonding with others.

A LONG WAY AND A SHORT WAY

Acquiring the quality of altruism is our purpose in life. We are pushed toward it by Nature's evolutionary law through egoism itself. Nature's purpose is for us to understand the required correction, and to complete ourselves by awareness and understanding, by agreeing with the process of changing our attitude toward others. Hence, each of us can choose between two paths:

1. Promoting ourselves in the evolutionary process by recognizing our egoistic Nature as harmful and as opposite to Nature's quality of altruism, and learn the method of correcting it.

2. Wait until blows, pressures, and suffering that stem from imbalance with Nature force us to look for a method to correct the imbalance against our will.

Correcting the ego by escaping pressures and suffering is guaranteed. But we are given the option of choosing the evolutionary process first, thus understanding and controlling the ego. In doing so, we will quickly and painlessly be balanced with Nature's common law—the altruistic law of giving and loving. These two paths of evolution are called "the path of correction" and "the path of suffering."

There is no question about Nature being the ultimate "winner," whose laws we will ultimately obey. But the question is, how will we choose to do it? If we prefer to march toward balance of our own volition, before suffering compels us to do it, we will be happy. Otherwise, hardships will impel us from behind and give us a different kind of motivation. Curiously enough, in Latin, the word for motive is *stimulus*, which is really a sharp stick that asses are poked with so they will walk more quickly!

It would seem that to experience the state of equilibrium with Nature, which is the best state that exists, we need to first experience its opposite state, the worst state that exists. This is so because we perceive things through two opposites: light compared to darkness, black compared to white, bitter compared to sweet, and so on.

However, there are two possible ways to experience the bad state. The first is to actually be in it, and the second is to picture it in our minds. This is why we were created as emotional and intelligent beings.

We can picture the terrible meaning of total imbalance between us and Nature without experiencing it physically, as it is written, "Who is wise? One who sees the future" (*Talmud Bavli*, Tamid, 32:1). If we imagine the worst possible state clearly enough before we reach it, the depiction will serve as a motivating force that can turn us away from future harm and toward goodness in due time.

By doing so, we will be spared tremendous suffering and we will accelerate the pace of our evolution. Disseminating the knowledge about the reason for all the crises and the problems, and the way to resolve them and head toward a new life, will hasten humanity's march on the path of correction.

CHANGING OUR ATTITUDE TOWARD OTHERS BRINGS ALL OF NATURE INTO BALANCE

We can easily see that changing our attitude toward others will lead us to the resolution of the problems on the social-human degree. This will mean the end of war, the end of violence and terrorism, and the end of general animosity among people.

However, the same crisis is occurring on Nature's other levels, too, in the inanimate, the vegetative, and the animate. What shall become of them? How will their situations improve? It would seem that to tend to the state of the Earth, water, air, flora, and animals, we must act directly on them. It is, therefore, surprising to see that Kabbalah's method of correction focuses on human relations and considers those relations the key to the state of all of Nature.

Can it be that correcting our human egoistic relationships will affect the state of other degrees, as well? Could it, for instance, resolve the ecological perils and the shortage of resources that threaten us?

We should know that Nature's altruistic force is a single force. There are no divisions in it. But with respect to us, it is divided into inanimate Nature, vegetative Nature, animate Nature, and speaking Nature. In other words, there are four different degrees of Nature affecting us.

At the inanimate level, it is affecting us through the Earth, for instance. At the vegetative level, we are affected through plants and trees; at the animate degree, through animals and through our own bodies; and at the speaking degree, through our social environment. However, it is all the same force, and only our senses, as we will later learn, divide it into many levels and numerous forces.

One reaches the highest point of equilibrium with the altruistic force by being of the same thought, desire, and intention. This level of balance is called "the speaking degree." If we love others, if humanity exists as one unit, and if we are connected to one another as parts of a single organism, we thus create equilibrium between ourselves and this force at the highest level.

For this reason, this force will be balanced in all the lower degrees as well. Thus, all the negative manifestations of imbalance—the suffering and the dearth we experience today at every level: inanimate, vegetative, animate, and human—will cease.

However, when we balance ourselves with respect to Nature's force at lower degrees than the speaking level, when we correct our attitude to the inanimate, the vegetative or the animate, we will still experience imbalance in those degrees. For example, if we relate lovingly to all of Nature's inanimate degrees and avoid destroying land, the ozone layer and so on, we will create a balance at the inanimate level. But at the vegetative, animate, and speaking levels, the imbalances will remain.

Hence, although Nature's force would treat us favorably, it would be a very small, limited change. If man treated Nature lovingly at the vegetative degree, too, this would certainly increase the balance with that degree. As a result, we would feel that our condition had grown a little more comfortable and easy. Similarly, if we were to behave in this way toward the animate degree in Nature, it would improve our condition a little more.

But all of the above is nothing compared to balancing the speaking degree. We human beings are the speaking degree. Hence, what must be balanced is the speaking degree within us.

This situation can be compared to an adult who approaches life from the perspective of a child, ignoring his or her talents and skills. By so behaving, the adult is not in sync with the way Nature treats each and every person: in accord with the evolutionary potential instilled in them, even if the individual is not realizing that potential.

Nature aspires to bring everything into balance, but this will be achieved only when man's attitude toward others becomes altruistic. Hence, the balancing law that propels all existing processes also goads us to be balanced, specifically at the speaking level. It does not allow us to have a secure, easygoing life using actions at lower levels.

Thus, until we create an altruistic bonding among all people, we will continue to experience a negative impact of Nature's force upon us. Because our senses divide Nature into different levels, we will also continue to create crises at all levels of reality. For this reason, while we are trying to cope with one problem, such as ecology, other problems will emerge from all sides, and ever more quickly.

We cannot allow ourselves to treat Nature's lower levels in hopes of escaping the real problem: correcting the egoistic relationships among people. The whole of Nature depends precisely on correcting our relationships. If we really want to improve Nature, working on our personal relationships is the way to do it.

Humans are the only creatures whose nature grants them an opportunity for free choice; that choice is only at the level of correcting human relations. The comprehensive balancing of all of Nature's degrees depends solely on our realization of this choice.

Everything that happens in the world depends on man alone. This is what *The Book of Zohar* explains (*Zohar*, Tazria, item 113). It states that everything exists and occurs for man, to help us form the right connection between ourselves and others, and acquire Nature's quality of altruism. This will bring the ultimate solution to all the world's problems, and all of Nature will exist in a corrected form, in harmony and in perfection.

In his manuscripts (p. 170), Rabbi Kook described this state in the following words: "The power of creation and global management has been executed in utter perfection... However, there is a small part that lacks correction... and upon its completion depends the completion of the whole created being. That tiny part is the human soul, in the form of its desire and in the mimicry of its spirituality. This part is given to man to correct, and with it, to complete the whole created being."

Nature's laws, as presented here, are hidden laws that Kabbalists discovered as they studied Nature in its totality. They indicate how to resolve all the problems of our existence. They cannot be proven, but they can be explained in a rational and compelling manner. In the end, after all the explanations, it is for the individual to decide whether or not to accept them.

And the reason this is so is that Nature wants us to maintain our independence, our ability to choose whether or not we want to strain to find where we are deflecting from the rules—a variation that causes us to feel Nature's impact on us as negative.

If things had appeared before us as solid facts, clear and unequivocal, it would rob us of the ability to choose freely, our only means of realizing our degree's unique potential. We would thus decline to be of the animate degree, completely operated by Nature's commands. Nature has placed us under such concealment to allow us to complement it by ourselves and build the complete speaking degree within us. If we make the most of our opportunity for free choice, we will succeed.

6

THE ROAD TO FREEDOM

Each of us perceives him or herself as an individual being, a unique, independently acting entity. It is no coincidence that for many centuries, humanity has been fighting to obtain a certain measure of personal freedom. The concept of freedom concerns all creatures. We can see how animals suffer when they are taken captive, when their freedom is denied. This is stark testimony to Nature's disagreement when any creature is enslaved.

Yet, our understanding of the concept of freedom itself is rather vague. If we examine it in depth, almost nothing will remain of it. Thus, before we demand an individual's freedom, we must assume that each individual actually knows what both freedom, and the aspiration for freedom, actually are. But first and foremost, we have to see whether the individual is even capable of acting out of free will?

Life is an endless war to find a formula for a better life. Did we ever ask ourselves what we actually controlled, and what we did not? Quite possibly, in most cases, things are mapped out to begin with, but we continue to behave as if the course of events depends on us.

The concept of freedom acts like a natural law that applies to all of life. This is why each creature aspires for freedom. Yet, Nature does not provide information concerning which actions we are free to choose, and which give us only the *illusion* of freedom of choice.

Thus, Nature places us in a state of complete helplessness, uncertainty, and disillusionment with our ability to change anything, either within ourselves or in life in general. Nature does that to make us stop the race of life and dedicate some thought to the question, "What *can* we influence?" If we know what elements shape us within and without, we will be able to understand the exact place where Nature allows us to control our destiny.

PLEASURE AND PAIN

Pleasure and pain are the two forces through which our lives are managed. Our inherent Nature—the desire to enjoy—impels us to follow a predetermined behavioral formula: the desire to receive maximum pleasure for minimum effort. Hence, we are compelled to choose pleasure and flee from pain. In that, there is no difference between us and any other animal.

Psychology recognizes the possibility of changing every person's priorities. We can be taught to perform different calculations of profitability. It is also possible to extol the future in the eyes of every person so that he or she will agree to experience present ordeals for future gain.

For example, we are willing to make tremendous efforts in schooling to learn a trade that will yield high wages or a respectable position. It is all a question of profitability calculations. We calculate how much effort will bring us how much likely pleasures, and if we are left with a surplus of pleasure, we act to achieve it. This is how we are all built.

The only difference between man and beast is that man can look forward to a future goal and agree to experience a certain measure of hardship and pain for a future reward. If we examine a specific individual, we will see that all actions stem from this kind of calculation, and that one, in fact, performs them involuntarily.

Although the desire to enjoy compels us to escape pain and choose pleasure, we are unable to choose even the *kind* of pleasure we will want. This is because the decision as to what to enjoy is completely out of our hands, as it is affected by others' desires.

Each person lives within an environment of unique laws and culture. Not only do these determine the rules of our behavior, but they also affect our attitudes toward every aspect of life.

In truth, we do not choose our way of life, our fields of interest, our leisure activities, the food we eat, or the clothing fashions we follow. All these are chosen according to the whims and fancies of our surrounding society.

Moreover, it is not necessarily the *better* part of society that chooses, but rather the *greater* part. In fact, we are chained by the manners and preferences of our societies, which have become our norms of behavior.

Gaining society's appreciation is the motive for everything we do. Even when we want to be different, to do something that no one else has done before or buy something no one else has, or even retire from society and seclude ourselves, we do it to gain society's appreciation. Thoughts such as, "What will they say about me?" and "What will they think about me?" are the most important factors for us, though we tend to deny and suppress them. After all, admitting to them would seem to annul our "selves."

WHERE DOES CHOICE COME IN?

From all the above, where, if any, do we find free choice? To answer this question, we must first understand our own essence and see which elements comprise us. In his essay, "The Freedom," written in 1933, Baal HaSulam explains that within each object and within each person are four factors that define them. To explain these factors, he uses the example of the growth of a wheat seed. This is an excellent example, as it is easy to follow its growth process and helps us to understand the whole concept.

1. The First Matter—Our Inherent Essence

The first matter is the inherent essence within every object. Although it may take different shapes, in itself, it never changes. For example, when wheat decays in the ground and its shape is completely lost, a new bud of wheat still grows from its inherent essence. The first factor, the essence, the bedrock, our genetic code, is within us from the very start. Hence, we are unable to change or affect it.

2. Unchangeable Qualities

The evolutionary laws of the essence never change, and from them stem the unchangeable qualities of each object. For example, a wheat seed will never produce any other kind of grain besides wheat; it will produce only the previous shape of wheat that it had lost.

These laws and the qualities deriving from them are predetermined by Nature. Each seed, each animal, and each person contains the evolutionary laws of the essence. This is the second factor that comprises us, and which we cannot affect.

3. Qualities that Can Be Changed By Affecting the Environment

While the seed remains the same kind of seed, its outer appearance changes according to the external environment. In other words, when affected by external elements and by defined rules, the "envelope" of the essence changes in its quality.

The influence of the external environment adds more elements to the essence, and together they produce a new quality of the same essence. These elements might be the sun, soil, fertilizers, moisture, and rain. They determine the difficulties the new wheat will meet in its growth, as well as its quantity and quality.

If we transfer this example to a person instead of a seed, the external environment might be parents, teachers, friends, colleagues, books, and the messages one absorbs from the media. Thus, the third factor is the laws by which the environment affects the individual and induces changes in those qualities that are changeable.

4. Changes in the Environment that Affect the Object

The environment that affects the growth of the wheat is, itself, affected by external elements. These elements can change drastically: for example, there might be a drought or a flood, causing all the seeds to rot or dry out. As for man, this fourth factor involves changes in the environment itself, which then change how it affects the changeable qualities in the individual.

Thus, these four factors define the general state of each object. These factors define one's character, mode of thinking and process of deduction. They even determine what one wants and how one acts at any given moment. In the essay, "The Freedom," Baal HaSulam discusses each of these factors at length and reaches the following conclusions:

1 One cannot change one's genetic code, one's essence;

2. One cannot change the laws by which one's essence evolves;

3. One cannot change the laws by which external elements affect one's development;

    4. One can change the environment one is
       in, and on which one is totally dependent,
       and choose a more favorable environment
       to attain one's life goals.

Put differently, we cannot affect ourselves directly, since we do not define our own essence and the way it develops. We are also unable to change the laws by which the environment affects us. However, we can influence our lives and our destinies by improving our environment. Thus, our only free choice is *the choice of the right environment.* If we induce change in our surrounding conditions and improve our environment, we will change the effect of the environment on our changeable qualities, and thus determine our future.

In all of Nature's degrees—the still, vegetative, animate, and human—only the human can consciously choose an environment that defines its desires, thoughts, and actions. Hence, the correction process is based upon the relationship of the individual with the environment. If our environment comprises a suitable basis for growth, we will reach splendid results.

7
REALIZING OUR FREE CHOICE

If we summarize the four factors that design us, we will see that in the end, we are ruled by two sources: our inborn elements, and the information we absorb from our environment during the course of our lives.

Interestingly, science has reached similar conclusions. Since the 1990s, the field of behavioral genetics has been gaining ground. This field of science seeks the links between genes and personality, and human cognitive and behavioral qualities, such as irritability, adventurousness, shyness, violence, and sexual desire.

One of the first researchers in this field was Professor Richard Abstein, head of the Research Department at the Herzog Psycho-Geriatric Hospital in Jerusalem, Israel. Prof. Abstein argues that genes determine about 50% of our characteristics, and the rest are determined by the environment.

Since we cannot change our innate structure, we must turn to the second element that our development depends on—our environment. The only thing we can do to progress toward realizing our life goals is to choose an environment that will push us toward it.

In "The Freedom," Baal HaSulam explains: "Therefore, one who strives to continuously choose a better environment is worthy of praise and reward. But here, too, not because of one's good deeds or thoughts, which emerge without one's choice, but because of one's effort to acquire a good environment, which brings one these good thoughts and deeds."

Those who strive to choose and create a favorable environment for the optimum development can thus realize their individual potential. Understanding this principle requires quite a bit of awareness, but apparently many today have already acquired it.

If we wish to turn our attitude from egoistic to altruistic, we must bring ourselves to a state where our desire to care for others' wellbeing and to bond with them is far greater than our desire for any egoistic possession. This can happen only if our environment's values affirm that altruism is the highest value.

We were made as social, egoistic creatures. Hence, there is nothing more important to us than the opinions of those around us. As a matter of fact, our life's purpose is to be praised and appreciated by society. We are completely and involuntarily controlled by society's views, and we are willing to do all that we can for its appreciation, recognition, respect, and fame. This is why society can instill a wide variety of values and behaviors in its members.

Society also constructs the criteria we use to measure our self-respect and self-esteem. Hence, even when we are alone, we operate according to society's codes. In other words, even if no one knows about a certain act that we perform, we will still perform it for the sake of self-appreciation.

To start building our desire to care for others and to bond among others as parts of a single system, we must be in a society that supports it. If people around us appreciate altruism as the highest value, each of us will naturally be compelled to obey and adopt it.

Ideally, our environment should project this: "To reach equilibrium with Nature, be good to others, to the single system of which you are part." When the desire for altruism is evident in our surrounding environment, we will absorb this value from it. If we encounter reminders and respect for altruism wherever we go, our attitude toward others will change. Gradually, the more we think about it, the more we will want to become healthy parts within the single system.

The environment can be likened to a crane that lifts us to a higher level. Hence, our first step toward meeting our life goals is to contemplate and search for the most suitable environment to support them. As we absorb the effects of being in the environment we chose, we will move more surely toward our objectives.

As we have said, the power of thought is the most powerful force in Nature. Therefore, if we aspire to be in a better environment, our innate force will lead us toward an environment where we can develop. The more we focus on improving our environment, the more possibilities will open up before us to implement it.

When our environment consists of people who are drawn to seek equilibrium with Nature, we will be able to use their examples and be encouraged and energized by them. These people will understand that we want to treat them with love, and will help us learn how to do it.

In this manner, through "practicing" on others, we will learn the meaning of being similar to Nature's force, and feel how good it is to be inside this love. In such an environment, we will feel protected, happy, and carefree. This is the kind of life toward which Nature is leading humanity.

IMITATING NATURE

We can begin our process of assuming Nature's qualities of loving and giving by making an effort to care for others, bonding with them with the recognition that all are part of a single body. Of course, this is still not an internal ego correction, but it is the first step in the process.

We can actually mimic Nature the way a child mimics its parent. Even though children do not understand what their parents do, they imitate them because they want to be like them. For example, a boy sees his father hitting a nail with a hammer, and imitates his father with a plastic hammer. By so doing, he gradually acquires his father's knowledge. If we try to imitate Nature's quality of love and giving, this mimicry will serve as a higher degree than ourselves, and we will want to reach it in our innate qualities as well.

Care for the wellbeing of others can arise from two motivations:

1. Wanting society's respect and appreciation.

2. Genuine acknowledgement of the supremacy of the quality of love and giving to others, over the quality of appreciating only oneself.

Imitating Nature the way a child imitates its father, without understanding quite what the father does, means caring for the wellbeing of others because of the first motive, not because of the second. Such mimicry is the basis for the mechanism of development and growth, and we cannot exist without it.

At first, we will care for others simply to receive the pleasure of social recognition. Gradually, however, we will begin to feel that such an altruistic attitude toward others is a sublime and extraordinary thing in and of itself, regardless of the social esteem it grants. We will find that an altruistic attitude toward others is a source of perfect, unbounded pleasure as we actually begin to feel Nature's force itself, the unlimited, unbounded perfect force.

In other words, through our efforts to imitate Nature's force, we will begin to feel that there is wholeness within Nature's quality itself. This feeling will induce an internal change within us; we will slowly realize that the attributes of loving and giving are sublime, nobler than our inborn attribute of self-reception, and we will want them.

In this manner, we will rise from the level we were created in, to a higher level, the level of Nature's force itself. We will be integrated in its harmony and perfection. This is where Nature's evolutionary law is leading humanity.

A NEW DIRECTION

At the moment one begins to balance oneself with Nature's force, the pressure for self-change lessens. This, in turn, reduces the negative phenomena in one's life. In fact, from Nature's perspective, nothing changes in this scheme; it is the individual who changes. Thus, the change itself creates in that person a sensation that the impact of Nature's force has changed.

Yet, humans are built in such a way that we feel that things outside us change, not us. This is how reality is perceived in human senses and in the human mind. In truth, however, Nature's force is constant and unchangeable. If we are identical to it, we feel wholeness. If we are completely opposite, we feel that this force is totally against us. In between these two extremes, we feel the intermediary stages.

Today, the contradictions between us and the altruistic Force of Nature are not 100% opposed to each other, since our egos have not reached their maximum level of development. This means that the level of negative phenomena we are experiencing is not at its potential worst. This, by the way, is also the reason some of us still do not feel the general crisis that the world faces.

But our egos grow daily, and they will intensify the contrast between Nature and us. To spare us the experience of the suffering this contrast entails, we should begin to advance toward acquiring the attribute of altruism, to change the course of evolution. And we should begin soon.

When we do, we will immediately feel a favorable response at all levels of existence. For instance, let us assume that a certain man has a son who is behaving very badly. The father talks to the son and tries to persuade him to change his ways. In the end, they agree that from now on they will begin with a clean slate, and the boy will better his ways. If, in the next day, the boy succeeded in improving his ways, even just a little bit, his father's attitude toward him will immediately change for the better. Thus, everything is measured and judged not according to the result, but according to the *direction*.

When more people become concerned about correcting interpersonal relationships, and regard this attitude as the most important thing, because their lives actually depend on it, their common worry will become public opinion, which will affect all the members of society. Because of the internal connection among us, everyone worldwide, even in the most desolate places, will instantaneously begin to feel that they are connected to all other people and depend on them. People will begin to think about the reciprocal dependency between themselves and the rest of humanity.

Various sciences, primarily quantum physics, provide proof that changes in one element affect other elements. In his book, *The Chaos Point: The World at the Crossroads*, Prof. Ervin Laszlo describes experiments that are routine in today's quantum physics. They show that particles actually "know" what happens to other particles, as though information about changes in other particles "traverses" every distance instantaneously.

Today, physics acknowledges that there is a constant reciprocal connection among particles, even when separated by space and time. This phenomenon pertains to all structures in the universe, from the smallest to the greatest.

Thus, today science is discovering that everything is inherent in the genes and the influence of the environment; it is helping us "wake up" from our illusions that "I determine and control," and "I examine and decide."

This unlocks a real opportunity to discover true freedom. We can come out from our slavery to our egos and acquire the quality of altruism by creating an environment that will help us imitate Nature, just as children learn from grownups.

The greatest researchers have always known that, as we become wiser, we discover the wondrous wisdom concealed in Nature. All our discoveries combined only make us realize that we are nothing but an offshoot of the unfathomable wisdom that exists, which opens up to us when we are ripe and ready to absorb it.

In Albert Einstein's words (quoted in his *New York Times* obituary, April 19, 1955): "My religion consists of a humble admiration of the illimitable superior spirit who reveals himself in the slight details we are able to perceive with our frail and feeble minds. That deeply emotional conviction of the presence of a superior reasoning power, which is revealed in the incomprehensible Universe, forms my idea of God."

8

EVERYTHING IS READY
(FOR LIFE'S PURPOSE)

EVOLUTION
OF THE GENERATIONS

Society today is an egoistic society. However, it also contains sufficient preparations that can help it become an altruistic society. As a matter of fact, the evolution of humanity throughout the generations was only made to prepare it to realize the purpose of life in this generation.

In the article "The Peace," Baal Ha Sulam describes the evolution of the generations as follows: "...in our world there aren't any new souls as the bodies are new, but only a certain amount of souls that incarnate on the wheel of transformation of the form, because they dress each time in a new body and a new generation.

Therefore, with regard to the souls, all generations since the beginning of creation to the end of correction are as one generation that has extended its life over several thousand years until it developed and became corrected, as it should be."

From generation to generation, the souls accumulate data, which eventually brings us to our present level of evolution. At the end of the long evolvement, the speaking (human) degree, should rise to a new level, which we will call "The Corrected Speaking."

To understand the impact of the evolution of generations before us, we can compare the internal data within us to units of information. Such units of information are within every object that exists in reality, and contain the innate data of all matter.

In truth, we are living in a space that contains an enormous amount of information about each and every element. This is an information field called "Nature's thought," and we exist within it. Any change that occurs in any element, such as efforts to maintain its present state, transition from state to state, forces operating on it, forces which it operates on other elements, internal changes, external changes, all those are changes in the information field.

In every generation, people look for a formula for balanced existence and a good life, the formula that Nature did not grant them. These searches are registered as additional records within their internal data units. As a result, these information units gradually improve.

All the understanding and the knowledge we acquire in one generation, through our efforts to have a better life and to cope with our environment, become additional natural inclinations in the next generation. Consequently, each generation is more developed than its former.

It is a recognized fact that children are always better able to cope with innovations than their parents, who actually invented those innovations. Today's toddlers, for instance, approach such things as cellular phones and computers very naturally, and require less time to learn how to operate them better than did their parents.

Thus, from generation to generation, humanity acquires knowledge and wisdom and evolves, much like an individual who has accumulated thousands of years of experience. In manuscripts published in the book, *The Last Generation*, Baal HaSulam writes about this accumulative process:

"The opinion of an individual is like a mirror, where all the pictures and beneficial and harmful actions are received. One examines all those attempts, selects the beneficial ones and rejects the acts that harmed one (called the "memory brain"). For example, a merchant follows (in the memory brain) all the merchandise in which one had lost, and the reasons; and similarly with all the merchandise and the reasons that yielded profits. They are arranged in one's mind like a mirror of attempts, after which one selects the beneficial and rejects the detrimental, until one becomes a good and successful merchant.

It is similar with each person in one's experiences in life. And in the same manner, the public has a common mind and a memory brain and common images, where all the actions performed with respect to the public and to the whole are registered."

The evolution of the information units within us has brought us to a preliminary level of awareness of just how opposite we are to Nature's force. Hence, we are becoming willing to listen to explanations of why we were created in this way. Moreover, we are becoming able to understand the goal we have to reach.

The internal void and the chasm being opened within many of us concerning the life we know are not coincidental. They are results of the creation of a new desire—for mankind to rise to a higher level of existence, that of the "corrected speaking. This is the evolutionary phase in which we can consciously advance toward the realization of life's purpose.

SOCIETY'S APPROACH TO ALTRUISM

Building an altruistic society will be widely supported by the public, since we all like to think of ourselves as good people who share other people's misfortunes and are helpful to others. This is how we are built. Theoretically, there is nothing to stop us from declaring that we are egoists and do not want to be considerate of anyone. But none of us is proud of his or her egoism.

Society naturally appreciates those who contribute to it. Hence, every person strives to be seen as such. Every person, society, public personality, or government wants to present itself as altruistic. Moreover, no individual will encourage others to be egoists, because that would be disadvantageous to oneself. For this reason, even the greatest egoists present themselves as altruists, not only to win society's appreciation, but to benefit from the altruism of others in return.

While it is true that there are highly unusual people who declare themselves egoists, they are not implying that they are proud of being detriments to society, but rather want to say, "Look at me, I'm special." With such a statement, they are merely trying to win society's attention.

Thus, no one openly objects to the expansion of altruism in the world. Some people will support altruism more actively and some more passively, but no one will be able to oppose it. Deep within, we all feel that egoism is killing everything and that altruism is a positive element that gives vitality and liveliness. This is why we teach our children to be considerate of others, even though we ourselves are egoists.

A NEW GENERATION OF CONFIDENT, HAPPY CHILDREN

Each of us strives to give his or her children the best tools for life. This is why we intuitively bring them up to be altruists. In fact, educating the younger generation has always been based on altruistic values.

We bring our children up to be kind to others because we subconsciously know that being unkind to others eventually hurts the unkind person. We want to give our children security, and we feel that we can succeed only by means of altruistic education.

Thus, a person's confidence does not depend on the individual, but on the environment. Because one's environment reflects a person's attitude toward it, all harm comes to us from the environment. However, by promoting altruistic values, we will increase the chances that society will not harm us.

Each society, in each country, throughout history, has wanted to impart altruistic values to its children. Only a very powerful individual, such as a tyrant whose army stands ready to enforce his will, can afford to teach his children to be ruthless, inconsiderate, and merciless. But the children of such people will need great protection to survive. They will have to stand guard against everyone else, and protect themselves through the force of arms.

A good attitude toward others imparts a sensation of security, peace and calm that is second to none. For this reason, we try to bring up our children with these values. However, and this is an important point, in time our children see that we, ourselves, are not behaving in this way toward others, and so they become as egoistic as we are.

Proper education is based on good examples. Are we showing our children an example of altruistic behavior toward others? The answer is probably negative, although we do bring them up to be altruistic when they are young.

A child who sees that his or her parents do not "walk the walk, but simply talk the talk," senses that their words are empty and false. As much as they will try to show their children the preferable way to behave, it will be useless.

The crises we are in today, and our perilous future, impel us to make a change. Thus far, we have been teaching our children to do one thing, yet did not follow our own advice. But now we have no choice. We must change our own egoistic attitude toward others.

As more and more people begin to behave altruistically, the reality that our children will be born into will change, and they will easily grasp what was difficult for us to understand. They will recognize that we are all part of a single system, and that accordingly, our relationships should be altruistic. There is nothing better that we can do for our children and for ourselves.

EGOISTS AND ALTRUISTS

Some individuals possess a natural inclination to help others. This is an additional preparation that exists in humanity for the correction process. Usually, the ability to empathize with others enables us to derive greater pleasure from contact with others.

However, some people experience others differently. They actually feel others' pain as though it were their own. Therefore, they are compelled to try and help others—at the same time relieving their own pain. These people are "egoistic altruists." For short, we will call them, "altruists," although they are, in fact, as much ego-centered as their fellow egoists who do not feel others' pain.

Egoists do not suffer from others' pain; hence, they may exploit them as they wish. Altruists, however, do suffer from others' pain; hence, they are cautious even of saying hurtful words. Both kinds receive these tendencies from Nature. Therefore, these differences do not reflect "good" people or "bad" people, but are simply evidence of one's obedience to Nature's commands.

It is possible to change a certain gene sequence to affect a person's ability to be good to others, Prof. Abstein discovered in his research of behavioral genetics. The researchers assume that there is a reward for altruistic behavior in the form of a chemical called "dopamine," released in the benefactor's brain and prompting a pleasant feeling.[18]

Approximately 10% of the world's population are this kind of "egoistic altruists." This is what Baal Ha-Sulam explains in the writings of The Last Generation, which cover his social doctrine and depict the shape of the corrected future society. Thus, humanity has always been divided into 90% egoists and 10% altruists.

Altruists care about the well-being of society, mutual aid in various fields, the well-being of the weak, and so on. In fact, altruists handle cases and situations that society does not, either for lack of attention or for lack of empathy with others' difficulties.

Altruistic organizations spend fortunes and make tremendous efforts in many ways; alas, for the most part, their help to the needy does not bring substantial changes to their situations.

Africa is an example of this state of affairs. In the past, before the West interfered with their lives, Africans provided for themselves. Today, however, despite the food and the water they receive, they are starving. The vast amount of money collected on their behalf does not change their situation; they are in constant struggle and are rapidly declining.

There is almost nothing that altruistic organizations have not tried to improve the state of the world. Still, the world's state is worsening. While it is possible to continue as we have been, it would be wise to take a brief pause and ask ourselves why we are not succeeding in improving the state of humanity.

The answer boils down to this: All the world's problems, personal and social alike, stem from man's imbalance with Nature. Accordingly, helping others on the material level may have short-term benefits, but in the long run these will fall away, as material aid does not promote mankind to balance, and thus does not resolve the problem at its root.

Of course, people should be fed when they are starving. But at the same time, after we have helped them get back on their feet and provided for their necessities, we must turn our attention to increasing their awareness of the true goal in life.

If we want to induce a positive change in the world and in ourselves, we must reexamine our definition of an "altruistic act," and make it more precise. Deeds should be measured by their overall contribution to humanity's genuine, fundamental change, and to uprooting human suffering at its source.

The situation can be compared to a person with a serious illness who takes tranquilizers instead of dealing with the illness itself. In the meantime, the disease worsens, and in the end, prevails. Actions that do not deal with the source of all our problems will not suffice, and will only postpone the outbreak of the illness in a much more severe form.

Acts are considered altruistic only if they intend to balance man with Nature's common law of altruism, if they elevate our awareness to the fact that we are all part of a single system, a single body that contains all people wherever they are, regardless of race or nationality. It is not about instinctive acts of charity to help people suffering from this or that distress. Rather, it is about actions carried out with the awareness of our urgent need to bring all of humanity, both weak and strong, into balance with Nature.

Hence, altruistic goodwill and energy should be channeled primarily toward raising humanity's awareness of why we have these problems, and how to resolve them. In this manner, the assistance given to us by Nature in the form of the ten percent of altruists in society will be wisely utilized, and their great potential realized.

The division into ninety egoistic percent and ten altruistic percent exists not only in humanity as a whole. It is also found within each person. One of reality's primary laws is, "General and particular are equal." It means that whatever exists in the whole also exists in each of its components.

The universe is holographic, as Michael Talbot demonstrates in his book, *The Holographic Universe*, a collection of scientific discoveries in that field. Baal HaSulam describes the same law in his own words in the article, "The Secret of Conception and Birth":

"General and particular are reciprocally equal as two drops of water, both in the externality of the world, that is, the general state of the planet, and in its internality. This is because we find a complete system of sun and planets dashing around it in even the smallest water-atom, just as in the big world."

This law shows that every person, whether egoistic or altruistic, consists of ten percent altruistic forces and ninety percent egoistic forces, as is the division in the whole of humanity. The difference between people is in the internal, individual state of these forces.

In an altruist, the (egoistic) giving force is active, and inactive in the egoist. But within each person exists an element of giving. Thus, there is not a single human being who lacks ability to reach equilibrium with Nature's altruistic force. After all, this is why these forces were planted in us to begin with. ✶

9

A REALITY OF WHOLENESS AND INFINITY

Where one thinks, there one is.

~The Baal Shem Tov

PERCEPTION OF REALITY

One who begins to realize everything described thus far, who contemplates being a part of a single system that incorporates all people, who transfers this knowledge to others and builds a supportive environment, gradually develops a powerful, genuine desire to acquire Nature's quality of altruism. The road to acquiring a complete desire for altruism is an adventurous one, and fills the lives of those who choose this path with deep meaning and unparalleled satisfaction. When the complete desire for altruism is built in a person, one discovers a whole new reality. Before we describe this reality and what a person who experiences it feels, we must understand what "reality" is, and how we perceive it.

These questions might sound redundant because it seems everyone knows what reality is. Reality is what I see, the walls around me, houses, people, the universe; reality is what we can touch and feel, what we hear, taste, and smell. This is reality—or is it?

Actually, there is more to reality than meets the eye, ears, and nose. Throughout history, the greatest human minds dedicated all their energy to this topic. Over time, science's approach to how we perceive reality has gone through several transformations.

The classic approach, whose chief proponent was Sir Isaac Newton, stated that the world exists independently, regardless of man. It makes no difference whether one perceives the world or not, or if there is a person living in the world or not. The world exists and its shape is fixed.

In time, the evolution of life sciences permitted the examination of the world-picture through the senses of other creatures besides man. Scientists learned that other creatures perceive the world in different ways. For example, a bee's world-picture is a sum of all the sights perceived in each of the myriad units that comprise its eyes. A dog perceives the world primarily as "odor patches."

Additionally, Albert Einstein discovered that changing the velocity of the observer (or the observed object), yielded a completely different vision of reality on the time/space axes. For instance, let's assume there is a pole moving in space. According to Newton, regardless of the speed, the pole will appear to have the same length in the eyes of an observer. According to Einstein, however, the pole will seem to be shrinking as its speed increases.

As a result of these two discoveries, a more progressive approach was formed, arguing that the world-picture depends on the observer. Observers with different properties and senses perceived a different world. Similarly, observers in different states of motion perceived a different picture.

In the 1930s, quantum physics revolutionized the world of science. It determined that the observer affects the event being observed. Accordingly, the only question the researcher can ask is, "What do the meters actually show?" It is pointless to try to research the objective process that occurred, or to try to find what the objective reality is like.

Discoveries in quantum physics, together with discoveries in other fields of research, combined to form the contemporary scientific approach to how we perceive reality: the observer affects the world, and thus affects the picture he or she perceives. Put differently, the picture of the world is a combination of the attributes of the observer and the attributes of the observed object. ◄

LIFE IS WITHIN

The current emergence of the wisdom of Kabbalah takes us one step forward. Thousands of years ago, Kabbalists discovered that, in truth, there is no such thing as a world-picture. The "world" is a phenomenon experienced within a person, and reflects the similarity between the individual's qualities and the qualities of the abstract force on the outside, i.e. Nature's force.

As we have said, Nature's force is totally altruistic. The measure of similarity or dissimilarity between one's attributes and the attribute of Nature's force on the outside, manifests itself as "the world-picture." It follows that the picture of our surrounding reality depends entirely on our internal qualities, which we can change completely.

To better understand how we perceive reality, we can compare a person to a closed box with five sensors: eyes, ears, nose, mouth, and hands, representing the five senses: sight, hearing, smell, taste, and touch. The picture of our surrounding reality is formed within this box.

Let us look at the hearing mechanism as an example of how our senses work. Sound waves that reach the eardrum create vibrations on its surface, which then move the hearing bones. As a result, electric signals are sent to the brain, which "translates" them into sounds and voices. All of our measurements take place from the eardrum inward, and all of our senses operate similarly.

Thus, we are not really measuring what is outside of us, but the response created within us. The range of sounds that we will receive, the sights we will see, the smells, all those depend on the sensitivity of our senses. We are "closed" within our box, and thus never know what really happens outside of us.

The signals from all our senses are summarized and transferred to the control center in the brain, where the received information is compared with the existing data in our memory, where previous impressions were collected. The information is then "projected" onto a "screen" within the brain, displaying the picture of the world we appear to occupy. This is how we feel where we are and what we need to do (see below drawing).

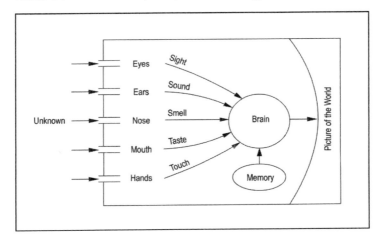

In this process, the unknown that surrounds us becomes something ostensibly known, creating an internal picture of what seems to be the outside reality. In truth, however, this is not the picture of the outside reality. It is only an internal picture.

All this has been known to science for a long time, and in his "Preface to The Book of Zohar," Baal HaSulam describes them in these words: "Take our sense of sight for example: we see a great world before us, and all its wondrous filling. But in fact, we do not see all that except in our own interior. In other words, there is a sort of a photographic machine in our hindbrain that portrays everything that appears to us, and nothing outside of us!"

He says that there is a kind of mirror in our brain, which inverts everything we see there to appear as if it is happening outside of us. Thus, the picture of reality is the upshot of the structure of our senses and the previously existing information in our brains. If we had other senses, they would create an entirely different picture. It is quite possible that what now seems like light would appear as dark, or even as something we cannot presently imagine.

In that regard, we should note that science has long known that it is possible to stimulate the human brain with electric impulses. These, combined with information collected in the memory, induce a sensation of being in a certain place and in a certain situation. Moreover, today we can replace our senses with artificial devices such as electronic instruments. There are numerous hearing aids, for example, ranging from amplifiers that assist those who are hard of hearing, to electrode transplants in completely deaf people.

An artificial eye is also being developed, using electrodes planted in the patient's brain. This "eye" inverts auditory data into visual data, meaning it changes sounds into pictures. Another development in vision healing involves planting a tiny camera in the eye that replaces the light waves that penetrate the pupil with electric signals. These signals are then transmitted to the brain, where they are "translated" into a picture.

It is clearly only a matter of time before we have full control over these health challenges, and can extend the range of our senses, create artificial organs, and even build an entire body. However, even then the picture of the world will remain an internal image.

As it turns out, all that we feel is only within us. It has no connection with the reality outside of us. Moreover, we cannot even say whether there is a reality outside of us, or not, since our picture of the "outside" world is within us.

NATURE'S PLAN

Our observations of Nature have shown that in order for life to form and continue, each cell in the organism and each part of the system must dedicate itself entirely to benefiting the body or the system it is in. At present, human society is not like that, which brings up the question, "How can we exist at all?" An egoistic cell in an organism becomes cancerous and its host body dies. We are egoistic parts in a single system, and yet we are alive!

The answer is that our lives are not actually defined as "living."

Man's existence is unlike any other degree in Nature in the sense that it is divided into two levels. The first level is the one we presently exist in. We feel separated from others; hence, we are inconsiderate of them and try to exploit them for our own benefit. The second level is the level of the corrected existence, where people function as parts in a single system, where they are in a state of mutual love, sharing, wholeness, and eternity.

Existence on the second level is defined as "life." Our current existence is a transition period designed to bring us to the point of attaining the corrected and eternal state by ourselves. Thus, Kabbalists, who have already climbed to the second level, define our current existence as "imaginary life" or "imaginary reality." When they look back to our level, they say, "We were like those who dream" (Psalms 126:1).

At first, the actual reality is hidden from us, we cannot naturally sense it. The reason is that we perceive our world according to our desires, our internal qualities. Thus, we presently do not feel that all people are connected as one because such a picture of relationships is repulsive to us. Our inborn egoistic desire to enjoy is not interested in this kind of relationship; hence, it does not allow us to perceive the actual picture of reality.

There are immeasurable elements we do not presently perceive. Our minds serve our egoistic desires, and operate our senses accordingly. This is why we cannot sense the existence of something that is not considered beneficial, or something to be wary of (in the context of an egoistic desire). If we can sense something, we sense it only if it is good for us or bad for us. Our senses are "programmed" in this manner and accordingly perceive the picture of our reality.

If we want to depict this picture correctly, we must now invert it to try to understand how reality is perceived through the eyes of an altruistic desire. Assume that we are beginning to be "calibrated" so we can sense what is good for others. In such a state, we will identify completely different things around us, from the things we previously noticed. Everything we saw before will seem completely different now. Kabbalists describe that state in the words, "an inverted world I saw" (Talmud Bavli, Pesachim, 50:71).

When we build within a new desire to be a healthy part in humanity, to be similar to Nature's altruistic force, this will mean the start of a new system of sensation, disconnected from our present system. This system will be called "a soul." Through the soul, one perceives a whole new world-picture, the picture of the *real* world, where we are all connected as parts of a single body, filled with eternal pleasure and bliss.

Thus, let us now refine and complete our definition of life's purpose, which we earlier defined as "bonding among people." Now, we see that the purpose of life is to consciously and willingly rise from the level of imaginary existence to the real level of existence. We must come to a state where we regard ourselves and reality not as we see them now, but as they really are.

In other words, the state we feel at present is an imaginary state in our egoistic tools of sensation. If we exert our efforts to progress with the correction process, and build within us a complete desire for altruism, our tools of sensation will become altruistic tools. And in them we will experience our state very differently.

Our actual state is an eternal state. We are all connected in a single system, and the flow of energy and delight within it is perpetual. In that state, there is recip-rocal giving; hence, the pleasure in it is infinite, perfect. In contrast, our present state is ephemeral and limited.

Our present sense of life stems from a tiny drop of vi-tality that trickles from the eternal state to our souls. This drop is a part of Nature's comprehensive altruistic force, which penetrates our egoistic desires, exists in them, and sustains them despite their dissimilarity with it.

The task of this drop is to sustain us in the first level of existence, the corporeal level, until we begin to sense the actual reality, the spiritual one. It follows that the present, transient lives we have are like a gift that has been handed us for a certain time, to be used as a means to reach the real life. In the real life, our sense of life will not be only that tiny drop, but the full force of Nature, the force of giv-ing and love, which will then be our life force.

The spiritual reality is not above us in the physical sense of the words. It is rather a qualitative discernment. To ascend from the corporeal reality to the spiritual real-ity is to elevate one's desire toward the quality of altru-ism, toward Nature's quality of love and giving. To sense spirituality means to sense how we are interconnected as parts of a single system, and to sense a higher degree of Nature. Life's purpose is to climb to the spiritual reality and experience it, in addition to our sensing of the cor-poreal reality, while we are living in a physical body, in the physical world.

By Nature's plan, humanity was created with the abil-ity to perceive only the first, imaginary level, and thus it evolved over the millennia. During that time, humanity accumulated observations and experiences that brought it to the awareness that an egoistic existence did not bring it happiness, and that it needed to switch to the second level, the "corrected altruistic existence." The overall crisis in the egoistic evolution places us at the transition point between the two levels of reality.

Hence, we must regard our days as a special point in time. We are at a turning point, moving toward a complete, eternal existence, which Nature had predetermined as the apex of human evolution.

Perhaps this is the time to explain that the pleasures we want today are very different from the pleasure that fills those who acquire Nature's quality of altruism. Today, we want pleasures from the sensation of ourselves as unique, special, superior. An egoistic desire can be filled only in comparison with a certain lack, either compared to a shortage that it previously had, or compared to others. Such pleasures require constant and rapid renewal, since the minute a pleasure satisfies a desire, it immediately cancels it, as we saw in Chapter Two. This process causes pleasures to be short-lived. When the ego intensifies, it produces a state where one can only feel satiation from the ruin of others.

An altruistic pleasure is quite the opposite. The altruistic pleasure does not *compare* with others, but is rather *within* others.

In a sense, we can compare this to a mother-and-child relationship. Because mothers love their children, they enjoy seeing them enjoying what they give them. The more a child enjoys, the more the mother enjoys, too. A mother feels joy precisely from those efforts she makes for her child, more than in anything else she does.

Naturally, such satisfaction is possible only on condition that we love the others, and its power depends on
our measure of love for them. Love, in fact, is the willing-
ness to care for the well-being of others, to serve them.
A person who feels that we are all individual parts of the
same system, sees service as one's role, one's sustenance,
and one's reward. Thus, there is a world of difference
between these two kinds of pleasure.

A person who has acquired the quality of altruism
has a "different heart" and a "different mind." Such a
person's desires and thoughts are so different from ours
that even his or her perception of reality is different from
that of others.

Thanks to the altruistic attitude to others, a person
abandons the sensation of being a single cell, connects
to the common body, and receives sustenance from it.
For such a person, the single system that we partake of
comes alive, and one begins to feel the eternal life of the
comprehensive Nature, the energy flow, and the endless
pleasure that fills the collective system.

Our sensation of life consists of two elements: reason and emotion. When a person feels and understands
the feelings and the reasons of the eternal Nature, one
then enters that world and lives within it. Such a person
stops regarding his or her life as something that is about
to end. Unity with the eternal Nature makes one's sensation of life continue even when one no longer has a life
in a biological body.

The death of the physical body means that the
body's perception of reality has stopped. The five senses cease to transfer information to the brain, and the

brain stops projecting the corporeal world-picture on the brain's "screen."

However, the system of the spiritual perception of reality does not belong to the level of the corporeal world. Hence, as soon as one acquires it, it continues to exist even after the demise of the body. Those who have sensed their existence in the spiritual system prior to death find that this sensation remains after the body has died, as well. This is the meaning of "living in one's soul."

The difference between how we now sense life, and the sensing of life that we *can* feel, is enormous. To try to describe it, *The Book of Zohar* compares it to the difference between the glow of a tiny candle and the radiance of infinite light, or between a grain of sand and a whole world. Obtaining the spiritual life is the realization of our potential as people, and this is what we should all reach while we are living in this world.

OPENING OUR EYES

Before we end this chapter, let's try a little exercise. Picture yourself in a completely dark room. It is so dark that you cannot see a thing. It is completely silent; there's not a sound, not a smell, not even something to touch. It's an empty, dark space. And you remain in that space for so long that you forget you ever had any senses at all; you even forget that such sensations exist.

All of a sudden, an odor arises. It grows stronger and surrounds you, but you cannot quite pinpoint it. Gradually, new scents join the first, some strong, some weak, some sweat, some sour. Now that you smell many scents, you realize that they come from different places, and you are in a space that contains directions such as right, left, above, and below.

Then, without warning, sounds appear from all around you, all kinds of sounds. Some are like music, some like words, and some like plain noise. Using the sounds, you can find your way in the world more easily. Now you can estimate distances, and guess the source of the smells and the sounds you are receiving. Now you have a whole world of smells and sounds.

After some time, you discover a new sensation as something touches your skin. Shortly after, you feel the touch of more things. Some are cold, some warm, some dry, and some moist; some are hard, some are soft, and some you can't decide. When some of these objects touch your mouth, you feel an odd sensation: they have a distinct flavor.

Now you are living in a world filled with sounds, scents, sensations, and flavors. You can touch other objects, and can learn about your surroundings. When you didn't have these senses, you couldn't even imagine that such a rich world was there the whole time.

This is the world of the blind-at-birth. Had you been in their shoes, would you feel that you needed the sense of sight, as well? Would you even know that you don't have it? Not at all.

In a sense, you may say that we don't feel the spiritual world for a similar reason, because we do not have a soul. We are living our lives without even knowing that there is a spiritual dimension that we are not sensing. We don't miss it. Our present world is quite sufficient. Day-by-day, year-by-year, and generation-by-generation we are born, live, enjoy, suffer, and eventually die. And through it all, we are not aware that a whole new dimension of life exists out there, a dimension of spiritual life.

And we would continue being unaware of it had it not been for the emptiness, the lack of meaning, and the apathy that have begun to surface within us. We no longer settle for realizing our desires because something else is still missing. Life as we know it and everything it offers is gradually becoming unsatisfactory. It is actually quite depressing, and so we choose to suppress these feelings. After all, what can we do? Everyone lives this way.

Actually, these sensations stem from the awakening of a new desire—a desire to enjoy something higher, sublime, above all that is around us, from a source unknown to us. If we really want to realize the desire that is now awakening in us, we will discover that this is a desire for something beyond this world.

The awakening of such a desire among many of us, as well as the growing sense of emptiness that accompanies it, are in fact natural steps, preordained in Nature's plan. This desire creates in us a sense that there is something beyond the familiar, and we are curious to find it. If we let this desire lead us and listen to the voice in our hearts, we will wake up to the real reality.[19]

10

BALANCE WITH NATURE

This chapter concerns a topic that is a little "off-track" from the topic of this book, but addressing it may help us clarify many of the topics discussed in this part of the book.

These days, when individuals and society are in a predicament, a new trend is spreading—the return to Nature. Some consider it a path towards change, and hope that it will improve their lives. But the question we must ask is, "Is there a connection between balance with Nature and return to Nature?" In other words, will returning to Nature help us achieve balance with it? This chapter will center on these questions and on similar topics.

The idea of returning to Nature is to live in harmony with Nature, much in the manner of our fathers and forefathers. Those who support returning to Nature strive for cleaner air, organic food production, and a return to country living. There are many aspects of this phenomenon, but they all center on the idea that if humanity were closer to Nature, we would be more balanced and, on the whole, feel better.

If we were to study how ancient tribes lived, we would find that the closer they were to Nature and to their roots, the more easily they sensed Nature's force of love. In that regard, I would like to mention a conversation I had with primatologist and anthropologist, Jane Goodall, who dedicated her life to the study of chimpanzees and lived among them for many years. For her research, she won numerous awards, including the Encyclopedia Britannica Award for Excellence, The National Geographic Society Hubbard Medal for Distinction in Exploration, Discovery, and Research, and the Albert Schweitzer Prize.

When I asked her about the discovery that impressed her most, she replied that after long years of living in Nature, she felt Nature's inherent force of love. She said that she began to feel and hear Nature, and that she felt love, that there was no "evil" force, only thoughts of love. Through long years of living in the jungle and merging with the primates, Goodall began to understand their emotions. She discovered that primates understand Nature and experience the love in it.

No doubt, such an experience is exciting. However, this is not the kind of balance we were referring to in this book. The most sublime feeling that the return to Nature can grant a contemporary person is a temporary and incomplete sensation of Nature's force of love. It is only a fraction of what every animal senses. However, Nature has designed for man a much higher degree of evolution than that.

There is good reason why Nature has pushed us out of the caves and the bush, and prompted us to develop human society with all its complex systems. It is precisely within the human society, atop the alienation and the intolerance of others, that we must create the balance between us and other people. We must use our own egos as levers to elevate us to that state. A return to Nature can be a fascinating experience, but it will not assist us in uprooting the problem we are suffering from—imbalance at the human level.

The return to Nature is often coupled with other traditional teachings such as Yoga, Tai Chi, and a variety of meditative techniques. Such teachings provide calm, peace, and a sense of wholeness. However, they cannot bring us closer to realizing Nature's goal, since they rely on suppressing the ego and diminishing it. In doing so, they lower the human ego from the speaking degree to lower degrees, called "animate," "vegetative," and "inanimate" degrees within man.

Therefore, these methods actually pull us back, and thus contradict the direction Nature is leading us in: elevating us to a higher level than our present state, to the level of the "corrected speaking."

Nature will not allow us to diminish our egos, as we can evidently see in countries such as China and India, which until recently maintained a low level of egoism, but are presently experiencing an outbreak of egoism. In recent years, they have joined the race for wealth and power and have closed a gap of many generations in record speed.

The egoism that is currently sweeping the world is the egoism of the speaking degree. To cope with it, a complete-ly different method must appear, a method whose inclina-tion is opposite from the inclination to decrease the ego. The wisdom of Kabbalah is the only method that utilizes the full force of the ego, while mending its application. It is surfacing today to help all of humanity realize Nature's goal and to rise as one to a new level of existence.

BALANCE AT THE SPEAKING LEVEL

For purposes of explanation, we will call the balance that relies on diminishing the ego from our present speaking degree to the animate, vegetative, and inanimate degrees, "balance at the animate degree." The difference between balance at the animate degree and balance at the speak-ing degree is on the level of how we sense Nature's force of love.

To equalize with Nature at the speaking degree, we must research ourselves and find where we, and all of humanity, are being led, the kind of evolutionary process we are in, its beginning and its ultimate purpose. With-out such self-scrutiny, under which we can experience every phase in this evolution, we cannot attain Nature's thought.

Such scrutiny can lead us to balance with Nature at the speaking level. In other words, it raises one to the degree of the corrected speaking. In that state, we can transcend the boundaries of time, space, and motion, and sense the entire flow of reality. The beginning of the process and its end unite, and we are aware of how all the phases in the process gradually surface within.

This allows us to perceive how all the phases are joined in wondrous harmony, how they are interdependent, and how they affect one another. Thus, one completes the evolutionary circle and no longer sees a beginning or an end in times, in places, or in processes, since one discovers that everything preexists in Nature's plan.

Attaining Nature's thought transcends us to exist at a supernal level, and grants us wholeness, eternity, and unbound pleasure. Our world is not where our bodies are, it is where our "selves" are. If we perceive a reality of eternity, sublimity, and perfection, this is where we are.

Attaining Nature's thought does not end with having a better feeling, but with having a sense of eternity and wholeness, as does Nature itself. Only in that state, the state of complete attainment, the corrected speaking, can one really feel why those who have attained Nature's force define it as one that is "good and does good."

While it is true that those who lower their egos from the speaking level to the animate level can feel Nature as benevolent, this would only be a sensation at the animate degree. In that state, they feel physically and psychologically contented, but this contentment is bound to be short-lived. Our egos incessantly grow and separate us from the animals; it will not let us settle for the animate state for long.

On the other hand, we might say that while animals feel the "good and does good" as a state, the speaking degree experiences it as a continuous process. The difference between the degrees is similar to the difference between one who feels contented detaching one's thoughts entirely and caring only for bodily pleasures, and one who uses one's mind and thinks about life from its start to its end. A person who thinks about life is in touch with an entirely different level of Nature.

One who reaches the sensation of the "good and does good" at the level of the corrected speaking regards life as more than mere contentment; rather, he or she is in touch with a higher reality, a flow of information and processes. Such a person enjoys the perception of Nature's wholeness. This liberates one from any limitation, and one ceases to identify one's self with one's body.

The thoughts of such people soar to a level of existence beyond the reality perceived in the physical senses, and reach into Nature's thought, the eternal, comprehensive field. Hence, when the body of such a person expires, one still feels that one's true self continues.

To summarize, the "return to Nature" is not connected to the spiritual process of achieving balance with Nature. It might even deflect our attention from the need to search for balance at the speaking degree within us, the level of thought.

The wisdom of Kabbalah, whose principles have been presented in this part of the book, specifies all the evolutionary phases we have experienced, and those we have yet to experience to reach Nature's goal. It explains that we are at the threshold of a dramatic change in people's awareness. Humanity will come to realize Nature's plan, there is no question about that. The only question that remains is, "How soon will it do so?"

PART TWO

Israel's Role

ISRAEL'S ROLE

The first part of this book explored both global and personal crises, their causes, and their resolutions. However, we cannot overlook some of the special issues of the state of Israel and the lives of each of its citizens. It is always surprising to see that such a tiny state attracts so much attention worldwide, and is continually at the center of colossal struggles.

Israelis are finding that, in their own homeland, personal and national safety are becoming fading dreams, growing dimmer with each passing year. Today, life in Israel is accompanied by constant fear: there is a bomb shelter around every corner, each apartment must, by law, have a "safe room" made of reinforced concrete, and security personnel search us at the entrance to every public place. In fact, throughout its lifetime, Israel has always been at war. Only its frontiers change their nature.

Today, in the era of weapons of mass destruction, accompanied by our neighbors' growing desire to destroy us, our very existence is at stake. The people are at the height of nervous tension. According to a survey published on the eve of Yom Kippur (Day of Atonement), 2006, "More than 50% of the residents of Israel are anxious about the very existence of the state. Two-thirds think it is plausible that a surprise attack on Israel will occur, as it did on Yom Kippur, 1973, and 70% do not trust the present political and military leaderships."

Moreover, we are not only failing to get along with the world, we seem to be torn and divided from within more than any other nation. We are split into sects that are hostile to one another.

Why is this so? Is there something special about us? Are we doomed to always suffer more than everybody else? Why are we not allowed to live our lives in peace? Why are the eyes of the world always on us? In this part of the book, we will clarify Israel's place on the "human map" and see if there is a way out of this bleak and ominous state. To do that, we will turn for assistance to the authentic wisdom of Kabbalah. Therefore, before we begin, let us study the origin of this wisdom, what it deals with, and how it relates to today's reality.

HUMANITY AND THE WISDOM OF KABBALAH

Man has always sought ways to be happy. Numerous teachings, old and new, try to provide it. However, humanity continues to suffer. None of the methods that mankind has developed throughout history yielded the craved happiness; hence, today people are losing interest in them.

It is at this time of bewilderment that a hitherto hidden method is now surfacing. Throughout history, its possessors have kept it hidden from the public eye. Nor was the general public attracted to it. But today it is bursting onto the center stage of the public agenda, and people throughout the world, from all nations, races, and nationalities are following it. This teaching is the wisdom of Kabbalah.

Millions around the world have the sense that by utilizing this method, they will receive the answers they have been seeking as to how they can be happy. This builds a strong attraction for people today. And, although most people still do not understand the essence of the method, they feel deep within that it will provide the answer. Thus, they are willing to explore what Kabbalah has to offer.

To understand what has made the wisdom of Kabbalah expand worldwide, we must go back to the cradle of humanity, to ancient Babylon, Mesopotamia. This is the beginning of the process that is being completed these days, a process that is attracting people to Kabbalah.

The wisdom of Kabbalah explains that the evolution of humanity is essentially the evolution of the desire to enjoy. This desire evolves from generation to generation and prompts us to fulfill it.

The first time a desire for something beyond the desire to exist appeared in a human being was 5767 years ago (according to the Hebrew calendar and to the date of writing these lines in 2006). Although many generations preceded Adam, he was the first person in whom the

The book, *Raziel ha Malaach, The Angel Raziel,* ascribed to Adam.

desire to comprehend the collective Nature appeared. It is not a coincidence that his name was Adam, because it comes from the words *Adamme la Elyon*, "I will be like the most High" (Isaiah 14:14). Adam was named after his desire to transcend his qualities and become similar to Nature's quality of altruism. Adam passed on what he had discovered to his offspring. Also, the book, *Raziel ha Malaach* (*The Angel Raziel*), is ascribed to him.

The day Adam discovered the spiritual world is called "the day of the creation of the world." This was the day on which humanity made its first contact with the spiritual world, and this is why the Hebrew calendar begins on this day.

According to Nature's plan, humanity will achieve balance with the inclusive Nature, the final correction of the human ego, within 6,000 years of this day. This is why it was written that "the world exists for six thousand years" (Talmud Bavli, Sanhedrin, 97:71). During those years, the human ego will gradually grow and bring humanity to the realization that it must be mended. It will also show humanity the method of correction, and how to implement it.

A few generations after Adam, humanity was centered around ancient Babylon, and that is where the first outbreak of egoism occurred. As a result, people began to want to dominate Nature and the world, and to exploit everything to their own benefit.

This outbreak of egoism was allegorically described as the building of The Tower of Babel: "Come, let us build us a city, and a tower, with its top in heaven" (Genesis, 11:4). However, the Babylonians' plot failed because it is impossible to satisfy the ego directly.

As their egos grew, it separated them from one another. Previously, the people of Babel had lived as one people. But now, when the ego began to "speak" in them, they stopped understanding each other. This moment is described as "the evolution of different languages." Thus, hatred drew them apart, and they were scattered all over the world.

Yet, in one of those Babylonians, a man named Abraham, there surfaced a desire to know the secret of life, along with the growth of the ego. It was the same desire that had first appeared in Adam.

Until that point, Abraham had been helping his father build idols and sell them. But once he began to feel that the idols no longer satisfied his growing desire, he began to search for higher forces. This story symbolizes Abraham's sensation that he was idolizing every egoistic desire he'd had, bowing before his desire and surrendering to its domination.

Thus, Abraham began to feel that such a life leads nowhere. He felt that if he wanted to transcend to a more highly evolved life, he would have to "break the idols" and to try to escape the ego's domination.

When he did, he discovered Nature's inclusive force and called it "God," which, in *Gimatria* (a method of using Hebrew letters as numbers), is equal to "the Nature."

Abraham realized that Nature's force necessitates all people to come into balance with it, and that the imbalance is the source of all suffering.

As Abraham continued to search, he discovered that the ego comprises 613 desires, each of which must be adapted to Nature's general law of altruism. In other words, in all one's desires, one must reach the state of "Love thy neighbor as thyself," the service of others.

When we correct each of the desires by using them altruistically instead of egoistically, Kabbalah calls this "performing *Mitzvot*" (keeping Commandments). This refers to changing the *intention* with which we use our desires, not to any physical actions.

The method for achieving equilibrium with Nature, beyond the ego, was discovered by Abraham. It is called "the wisdom of Kabbalah." *Sefer Yetzira (The Book of Creation)* is also ascribed to Abraham.

Abraham began to teach this wisdom to his people, the ancient Babylonians. It was written that "Abraham the Patriarch would bring them into his home, give them food and drink, and would bring them closer" (Bereshit Raba 84:4). However, most of the people did not take interest in correcting their egos.

But after Abraham and his wife, Sarah, made considerable efforts to teach the correction method, they managed to organize a group of people that became the first group of Kabbalists in human history. This group later received the name, "Israel."[20]

From that point on, humanity has been divided into two paths: Kabbalists and the rest of humanity. As the ego continued to grow, both among the Kabbalists and in the rest of humanity, it evolved very differently in each of these groups. The Kabbalists strained to maintain balance with Nature atop the growing ego, while the rest of humanity searched for new ways to satisfy their egos.

From generation to generation, humanity reached greater achievements. People kept believing that very soon they would reach their ultimate fulfillment. Yet they remained emptier than before the new hope had emerged. Today, the ego has reached its final degree; hence, many are sensing that millennia of the evolving ego have yielded only helplessness and a general, global crisis.

Realizing this puts humanity in the same position it occupied in Babylon. But this time humanity, which has spread across the globe and proliferated into billions of people, is ready to listen. Now, the time is ripe to absorb the method founded by Abraham, intended to teach everyone how to use their egos correctly, how to achieve balance with Nature, and how to feel like the whole of Nature: eternal and whole.

Until recently, Kabbalists were compelled to conceal this method from humanity. They had to wait until the final degree of the ego appeared, a level that humanity would despair of fulfilling. They waited for a time when people needed a correction method, and would feel that of all teachings, the cure for all ailments could be found specifically within the wisdom of Kabbalah. But now that these conditions have been met, Kabbalists, who carefully hid the method in the past, are opening it to all. This completes the historic cycle, and all of humanity as one body can now achieve equilibrium with Nature.

In a manifesto called "Messiah's Horn," Baal Ha-Sulam says that redeeming the world from its plights depends solely on disseminating the correction method: "We are in a generation that is standing at the very threshold of redemption, if we will only know how to spread the wisdom of the hidden in the masses."

He emphasizes that the wisdom of Kabbalah must be brought to everyone in the world, and compares it to the voice of the *Shofar* (a ram's horn blown on Jewish holidays): "And the dissemination of the wisdom in the masses is called "a *Shofar*." Like the *Shofar*, whose voice travels a great distance, the echo of the wisdom will spread throughout the world..."

THE BIRTH OF
THE PEOPLE OF ISRAEL

For the correction method to appear today and lead the world to equilibrium with Nature, it had to be passed on and developed from generation to generation. It is a process that began in the same group of Kabbalists that Abraham began, and has stretched over thousands of years.

After using Abraham's method for several generations, the intensified ego appeared in his group, too. In that state, to cope with the new egoism, it needed to find a higher level of the method of achieving balance with Nature.

The provider of this new method was Moses, the great Kabbalist of that time. Moses led the people out of Egypt, out of the domination of the new ego, and taught them to be "as one man in one heart," as parts of a single body. Because of its size, this group was now called "a people" or "a nation." However, genetically, it was part of the ancient Babylonian people to which Abraham belonged, as even science confirms today.[21]

Moses' method of balancing with Nature was a continuation of Abraham's method. It was named "The Torah." This does not refer to the Torah (Pentateuch) as a historic document, as we know it today, but as a method for correcting the ego. The term, "Moses," symbolizes the force that pulls (*Moshech*, in Hebrew) one out of the ego's rule. The term, "Torah," comes from the word, "instruction" or "light," the force that corrects, as in, "The Light in it reformed them" (Midrash Raba, Eicha, Introduction, 2nd paragraph). Torah also stands for the pleasure that fills one who has corrected one's ego.

Thus, the group of Kabbalists continued to evolve. Implementing Moses' method, they corrected all the egoistic desires that surfaced in them, and the filling (satisfaction, light) they received within their corrected desires was called *Beit ha Mikdash* (The Temple, The House of Holiness). The Temple is their corrected desires, which has now become a house filled with holiness; i.e., the quality of altruism, the quality of the comprehensive Nature.

As children were born, they were raised by the correction method and achieved their own spiritual attainments. Thus the people lived within the sensation of the common, collective Nature, until the ego jumped one more degree, causing them to lose that sensation. The detachment from the sensation of the inclusive Nature is called "the ruin of the Temple," and the new domination of the ego is called "the exile in Babylon."

The correction of the ego that erupted at the ruin of the First Temple was called "the return from the exile in Babylon and the erection of the Second Temple." However, this time the nation had been split in two: some succeeded in correcting their egos; others were overpowered by their egos and could not correct them. The ego gradually grew among the first group, too, until the entire nation lost the sensation of the inclusive Nature, and the people fell into spiritual concealment. This domination of the ego was called "the ruin of the Second Temple," and the people went on another exile, which was to be their last.

The ruin of the altruistic quality caused the entire nation to lose the sensation of the comprehensive Nature, except for a chosen few, the Kabbalists, who live in every generation. Away from the public's eye, these Kabbalists continued to develop the method to correct human nature and to adapt it to the growing ego. Their task was to prepare the method for a time when Israel and humanity would need it.

THE EVOLUTION OF
THE CORRECTION METHOD

Around the time of the last exile, in the 2nd century CE, *The Book of Zohar* was written by Rabbi Shimon Bar-Yochai and his disciples. The book describes both the correction method, and everything that one who achieves balance with Nature will experience. It also reveals every state that humanity will experience until the final correction of the ego. However, it uses intimations and allegories to do so.

It should be pointed out that even though *The Book of Zohar* was written before the people went into exile, it states that this book will be discovered only at the end of the exile. That is, its arrival will bring with it the end of the spiritual exile: "...because Israel is destined to taste from the *Tree of Life*, which is this book of Zohar, in which they will come out of the exile with mercy" (*The Book of Zohar*, Parashat Naso, item 90).

The *Zohar* also writes that toward the end of a 6,000 year period allotted to the correction of the ego, the book will be revealed to all of humanity: "When it is near the days of the Messiah, even infants in the world are destined to find the secrets of the wisdom, and to know in them the ends and the calculations of redemption. And at that time it will be revealed to all." (*The Book of Zohar*, Parashat VaYira, item 460).

Thus, immediately after it was written, *The Book of Zohar* was concealed. The next time the book appeared was in 13th century Spain. Then, in the 16th century, about 1,400 years after the writing of the *Zohar*, the Ari (Rabbi Isaac Luria) appeared in Zephath, a city of Kabbalists in the north of Israel. In a systematic, scientific language he revealed the *Zohar's* correction method. He also described in great detail the phases of the correction of the ego, leading to balance with the comprehensive Nature. His writings contain depictions of the structure of the Higher World, and explain how one can be admitted into that dimension of reality and live within it.

However, since the ego had not yet fully manifested its power during the Ari's lifetime, only few could understand him. This is because keener perception arrives when the ego is more evolved.

As the end of the correction period arrives, it brings with it the final level of egoism. And with this come the crises that create the necessity of the method to correct the ego. Today, many already need the full correction method, and they can grasp what very few could grasp in the past. This is why the complete method of correction has now been exposed.

Baal HaSulam (1884-1954) interpreted *The Book of Zohar* and the writings of the Ari so that each of us would be able to understand them. In "The Teaching of the Kabbalah and Its Essence," he wrote, "I am happy to have been born in such a generation when it is already permitted to publicize the wisdom of truth. And if you ask me, 'How do I know that it is permitted?' I shall reply that it is because I was given permission to disclose."

Baal HaSulam's primary compositions are *The Sulam Commentary on The Book of Zohar*, in which he translated the *Zohar* from Aramaic to Hebrew, and interpreted the words of the *Zohar*. He also wrote *The Study of the Ten Sefirot*, in which he described the writings of the Ari.

In addition to these enormous works, Baal HaSulam wrote many essays that clarify how to establish a human society that is balanced with Nature. He explained he was able to do so in response to that generation's need for a clear, systematic method to correct the ego.

"My whole merit in the way of the disclosure of the wisdom is because of my generation" ("The Teaching of the Kabbalah and Its Essence").

As Kabbalists predicted, the end of the 20th century saw the beginning of a new era in human evolution. Now, masses of people have become drawn to Kabbalah. Back in the 18th century, the Vilna Gaon pointed to 1990 as the year when the process of mass correction would begin, as it was written in his book, *Kol ha Tor (Voice of the Turtledove)*. Baal HaSulam named the year 1995 in a conversation with disciples in 1945.

It is no coincidence that interest in Kabbalah is unfolding in this manner. Kabbalists explain that if we wait until the end of the 6,000 years without progress in correcting our egos by ourselves, we will suffer tremendously, the majority of the world population will be extinct through horrendous wars, and the few survivors will still have to carry out Nature's plan.

In the writings of the last generation, Baal HaSulam explains that, "the Creator eventuated and gave humanity technology, until they have invented the atom and the hydrogen bombs. If the total ruin that they are destined to bring is still not evident to the world, they can wait for a third world war, or a fourth one and so on. The bombs will do their thing and the relics after the ruin will have no other choice but to take upon themselves this work."

In other words, if we say, "*Que sera sera*," and simply sit by without acting, Nature will force us to correct through dreadful pains within the framework of the remaining 233 years until the end of the 6,000 years. This painful process is called "in its time," meaning "in the time allotted."

But the suffering will intensify and increase until each moment seems like an eternity, as time is a psychological matter. In fact, we can already feel that our lives are getting increasingly harder, and this is just the beginning.

However, in the path of correction, there is no time limit. Just as Kabbalists throughout time achieved balance with Nature, anyone today can do the same and experience the same perfection and eternity. This path is called, "I will hasten it," because it accelerates time. One way or the other, we must all achieve balance with Nature, and even death is no escape from the mandatory correction process.

The choice between the two paths depends on our awareness, which will evolve either through suffering or through scrutiny. Evolution through scrutiny can be done using the wisdom of Kabbalah, which describes our situation, explains where we should reach, and provides the means to get there. Thus, it is possible that humanity will experience 233 years of unbearable torment as is described about the days of the Messiah in the Kabbalah books. Or this can be done in a much shorter time in boundless elation. At this crossroads, Israel's role is critical.

THE ROLE OF ISRAEL

The descendants of Abraham's group of Kabbalists are the people of Israel. Before we begin to discuss the role of Israel, it is important to know that there is absolutely no question of nationalism here, as Baal HaSulam puts in his essay, "Matan Torah" (The Giving of the Torah): "Is there, God forbid, nationalism involved here? Of course, only an insane person would think that." The people of Israel is no better than other nations, but it does possess a unique role in Nature's plan. Humanity is like a single body, where each of the organs has its own function.

Kabbalists allegorically say that in the beginning, the correction method was offered to every nation, since "the purpose of creation lies on the shoulders of the whole human race, whether black, white, or yellow" (Baal HaSulam, "The Bond"). However, when the Torah was given, none of the nations were ready to receive it; clearly, humanity did not need it yet. For this reason, the method was given to the people of Israel to function as a "transit" for the method that would ultimately be realized by all of humanity.

The people of Israel are different from all other nations. They comprise the same group of Kabbalists that Abraham established from residents of Babylon. Their task is to preserve the correction method throughout human history until the time when everyone needs it. At that time, this group, by now called "the people of Israel," would be able to realize its function and transfer the correction method to all the nations.

The fall of that group of Kabbalists under the ego's domination produced within them a sophisticated and unique ego. This was effected so the Jews would speed up the evolution of the world while they were still among the nations.

The nations of the world did not possess sufficient drive for progress, and the Jews' role was to urge them forward to greater egoistic evolution. Hence, Jews led the cultural, scientific, economic, and technological revolutions. These would accelerate the realization that egoism only brings the world to a dead end, and that we must correct it. Today, along with our awareness of our need to correct the ego, we should learn how to implement the correction method.

There are different phases in this process. First, the people of Israel must correct themselves and regain balance with Nature, which they lost some 2,000 years ago. For this to unfold, they must come to know the correction method they have been detached from, and begin to use it. Once they do that, they will serve as an altruistic example to the whole of humanity, and will fulfill their role of being "a light of the nations."

When the correction of Israel is transferred to the rest of the world, the second phase in the plan will be realized: the correction of all of humanity. Thus, "When the Children of Israel are complemented with the complete reason, the fountains of intelligence and knowledge shall flow beyond the borders of Israel. They will water all the nations of the world, as it is written (Isaiah 11), 'for the earth shall be full of the knowledge of the Lord.'" (Baal HaSulam, "Introduction to the Tree of Life," item 4).

THE RETURN TO THE LAND OF ISRAEL

The return of the people of Israel to the land of Israel is predetermined in Nature's plan. To understand it, we must understand the spiritual meaning of the term "the land of Israel." And for this, we must understand the language that Kabbalists use.

When Kabbalists achieved balance with Nature, they discovered a part of reality that is beyond the range of the egoistic person's perception. They called that part "The Upper World," or "The Spiritual World." Once they discovered that every element in the Upper World hangs down to our world and begets a corporeal manifestation, they called the elements in the Upper World, "roots," and their manifestations in the corporeal world, "branches." Thus, the "language of roots and branches" came to be, based on the parallels between the Upper World and our world.

In the language of the branches, "land" means "desire," and "Israel" means *Yashar El* ("straight to God"). Thus, "the land of Israel" designates a desire geared toward an altruistic action.

The generations that lived in the land of Israel before the ruin of the Second Temple were in a state of spiritual attainment. At that time, there was congruence between the spiritual degree of the people of Israel and its physical presence in the land of Israel, hence, Israel merited being there. As the people lost their spiritual degree and declined under the domination of egoistic desires, the incongruence between the spiritual level of the people of Israel and their presence in the land of Israel, eventually prompted the ruin of the Temple and the exile from the land of Israel.

While in the past their spiritual decline preceded the exile of the people of Israel, to go live among other nations, today the situation is reversed. The physical return of the people to the land of Israel preceded their spiritual return, but the congruence between the spiritual root and the corporeal branch must be rebuilt. The people of Israel must climb by the same path they previously descended, but in the opposite order: the physical return first, the spiritual return second.

Hence, the people of Israel are obligated to achieve the spiritual degree of "the land of Israel," and this is why the correction method is being revealed to them. As long as Israel is not corrected, its people will feel uncomfortable in that land. It is impossible to live in Israel without having a spiritual ideal; Nature's forces simply do not allow one to be at rest in that land, without the spiritual congruence.

To encourage the residents of the physical land of Israel to rise to the spiritual level, called "the land of Israel," reality appears unsafe and disquieting. All the pressures applied on Israel by other countries, as well as through internal social crises in politics, in society, and even in people's personal lives, are there to compel us to advance toward the goal of our existence in this world.

"In a sentence: As long as we do not raise our goal above the corporeal life, we will have no corporeal revival, because the spiritual and the corporeal in us cannot live in one basket, for we are the children of the idea" (Baal HaSulam, "Exile and Redemption").

The Book of Zohar and Kabbalists through the generations have declared the return of the people of Israel from exile as the time when the correction of the world would have to take place. Therefore, when the nation returned to Israel, the great Kabbalist, Rav Abraham Isaac HaCohen Kook, who was also the first chief rabbi of Israel, was very outspoken:

"Now the times have come for everyone to know that the salvation of Israel and the salvation of the entire world depend solely on the appearance of the wisdom of the hidden light of the internality of the secrets of the Torah (Kabbalah) in a clear language" *Letters of the Raiah*, p. 92). "Only when we are what we should be will humanism return to humanity, the highest virtue, whose essence will be able to the spiritual light concealed within its quality; and it will naturally soar in its entirety, and with pride it will know its happiness" *Sefer Orot (Book of Lights)*, p. 155).

We should know that just as the people of Israel are not counted among the seventy nations of the world, but are considered a special group intended to pass the correction method to all of humanity, "the land of Israel" will not exist on Planet Earth unless it is a land where a spiritual nation resides. Therefore, the people of Israel deserve to live in that land only to the extent that they perform their duty. Otherwise, they will not be considered "the people of Israel" and the land will not be considered "the land of Israel." Israel will then become a land that ejects and repels this people, a land that cannot stand this nation on its soil, "a land that devours its inhabitants" (Numbers, 13:32).

Baal HaSulam predicted that if no changes were made, the very existence of the Jews in the land of Israel would be at risk. In the writings of *The Last Generation*, he wrote that matters could deteriorate and so many would leave Israel that "bit-by-bit, they will escape the discomfort until too few remain to merit the name "State," and they will be swallowed among the Arabs."

UNITING THE NATION

If we really want to be a free nation in our land, as our national anthem states, we must implement the same formula that sustained us prior to the ruin and the exile. In place of the separation, alienation, and unfounded hatred that abound today, we must once more be as parts of a single body, and unite with the inclusive Nature.

And the means to achieve this unity atop our hefty egos is to implement the correction method.

In truth, we have gathered in the land of Israel primarily due to necessity. Nature's plan made the nations of the world pressure us, and compel us to escape from the Diaspora to find a haven in Israel. For the most part, people were made to come here as a place of refuge where they could be saved from the pressure of their enemies, or improve their corporeal lives. They did not come to Israel because of an internal drive to bond with love, create a united nation, balance with the altruistic Nature, and then lead all of humanity toward it.

In the end, our present ties will not enable us to face the nations that stand against us, whose internal bonding is much more solid than ours. Our foes are clearly aware of our weakness, as Zeev Magen, PhD, head of the History of the Middle-East department at Bar Ilan University explains[22]: "The Iranians and the rest of the fundamentalists are convinced that we are a society devoid of any infrastructure of uniform principles. Moreover, they are convinced that we have already concluded that such an infrastructure cannot exist. Therefore, the fundamentalists are positive that sooner or later they will defeat us and drive us out of here, or at least end our sovereignty. Certainty always overcomes uncertainty. Hence, in their eyes, we are living on barrowed time. A newspaper article recently published in one of the Arab newspapers, ended in a quote from Haminai, who was quoting from the Quran when he said that 'The Jews will not fight you as one man. You think that they are united, but their hearts are divided.'"

Unity among us can only be achieved when we unite around the realization of our duty to the world. We are not meant to bond in order to improve our situation at the expense of other nations or countries. The "nationalistic" idea of the nation that the wisdom of Kabbalah talks about is as far from "traditional nationalism" as the East is from the West. We must not regard ourselves as superior to others.

Quite the contrary, The "chosen people" means that this people was chosen to *serve all* the nations. Its duty is to help them achieve equilibrium with Nature, and to reach the degree of the greatest spiritual prosperity. We must regard ourselves as a means towards that end and nothing else; and we will only be able to perform it by achieving unity among ourselves.

Our return to Israel under threat was part of Nature's plan, and thus gave us the opportunity to discover for ourselves our inner need to unite, and to create a nation that leads humanity to wholeness.

It is no coincidence that we are currently failing to create a united society in Israel. We are divided into sects: secular vs. religious, left vs. right, Ashkenazi vs. Sephardic, natives of Israel vs. new *Olim* (immigrants) and so on. All our efforts to unite have thus far been futile; the social gaps are deepening, and hatred and alienation worsen. A recent survey disclosed that even today, 57% of the

Israeli public believes that the state of Israel's existence might be in danger due to unfounded hatred.[23]

In this present state, we must pause and find our roots, see where we come from, how we have become "the people of Israel," find the principles upon which the nation was founded and their purpose. Only when we actually "live" the eternal foundations of the spiritual ideals on which the state of Israel was founded will we be able to unite and to promote the unity of all people, wherever they are.[24]

ANTI-SEMITISM

No calamity comes to the world but for Israel.
~Talmud Bavli, Yevamot, 63:1

Understanding the role of Israel makes it easier to understand the phenomenon of anti-Semitism, and how it may be resolved. The root of both anti-Semitism and of blaming the Jews for every adversity that occurs in the world is part of the purpose of Israel's existence: providing the world the method for the correction of the ego. The fate of the people of Israel depends on the way they realize their task.

As long as Israel does not carry out the correction method on themselves and does not pass it on to the rest of the nations, humanity's imbalance with Nature will increase. This will go on to increase the intensity and frequency of negative phenomena in all of humanity, and in the lives of every individual. Today, these phenomena have worsened to the level of a global crisis.

Anti-Semitism is appearing in the world according to the evolution of the nations. Subconsciously, the nations sense that they depend on Israel for their happiness. This is why the negative attitude toward Jews has appeared specifically in more evolved nations. It is not surprising that Germany, the most developed country in the beginning of the 20th century, was also the country where a horrendous outbreak of anti-Semitism occurred. The more a nation's ego evolves, the more powerfully is awakened a hatred of Jews. In some, it is a violent reaction; in others, it is quiet consent and support.

Today, the evolution of the ego has made most of the world's nations resentful toward Israel. Even countries that were previously sympathetic toward Israel, such as North European countries, have changed for the worse. Surveys held in the European Union indicate that 60% of the population in the European Union believe Israel is the country that poses the greatest danger to world peace. In the Netherlands, for example, this view is supported by 74% of the population. The survey also revealed that Israel's image among the educated is deteriorating.[25]

Moreover, seemingly "small and insignificant" countries are making public anti-Israeli statements. Even countries that have no direct contact with Israel display anti-Semitic attitudes. All these phenomena are rooted in the Nature of Creation, as it is written, "It is known that Esau is hateful of Jacob" (Midrash Sifrey, Parashat BeHaalotchah, par. 11).

It should be pointed out that other nations relate to one another very differently from the way they relate to Israel. Even when two nations hate each other, they will unite under a common threat, just as animals cooperate to escape danger. But other nations' attitudes toward Israel are different: even under threat. They point the finger at us as the reason for their perilous state.

At present, many nations believe that there is no place for the people of Israel in the world, not even in the state of Israel. Such beliefs stem from an instinctive sense that we are the source of all predicaments. However, even these nations cannot consciously explain that to themselves or to us.

In fact, Jews, too, cannot understand why everyone hates them, and why they feel oddly guilty. It is almost as if they were indebted to the other nations, recognizing that they deserve this distinctive, negative attitude.

In fact, anti-Semitism does not depend on the nations of the world, but only on Israel's function. We must not rely on any one nation to assist us, or hope that the world's approach toward us will change for the better. On the contrary, hatred toward us will arise even in countries that today seem supportive of us, unless we begin to realize our destination.

THE RISE OF THE ISLAM

Besides increasing anti-Semitism, there is another recent phenomenon that is strongly affecting our situation: Christianity is surrendering its domination to fundamentalist Islam. This process is described in *The Book of Zohar* as part of the processes that will occur when Israel returns to its land: "And the children of Ishmael are destined to evoke great wars in the world, and the children of Edom will gather over them and they will wage war with them" (*Zohar*, VaEra, item 203).

When we study the rise of Islam, as when studying any process, we must first know that everything that happens in this world is a consequence of the balance of reality's hidden forces. For example, we cannot sense the force of gravity; we cannot see or feel it, but we *can* sense the consequences of its actions. We measure its effects and thus learn how to handle it.

In much the same way, there are forces in reality that affect human society. However, unlike forces affecting lower degrees than the human level (the still, vegetative, and animate in Nature and in our bodies), we cannot clearly identify the forces that affect human society, or their consequences. This is so because researching a certain phenomenon requires observing it from a higher perspective. For example, a child cannot study what it means to be a child. Similarly, we cannot presently understand the forces that affect our degree, the human level.

However, since reality is complete, just as natural forces affect all of Nature's degrees, human society is influenced by Nature's forces, even though they are hidden from us. In fact, all of the phenomena we observe in human society, in human relations, among peoples or among countries, are the effects of Nature's forces, which manipulate human society as a shepherd leads a herd.

If we want to change our situation, we must understand these forces and affect the place from which they affect us. And the degree from which they affect us is above the human level, hence it is called "Nature's Upper Level" or "The Upper World."

Kabbalists describe this *modus operandi* in the following words (Bereshit Raba, 10, 6): "There is not a blade of grass below that does not have an angel (force) above it that strikes it and tells it: 'Grow.'" In other words, nothing changes in our world without a force that operates it from a higher degree, the Upper World.

Therefore, to understand the relations among religions in general, and the rise of the Islam, in particular, we must know the Upper Root of religions: the three lines. In fact, man's evolution toward equilibrium with the inclusive Nature unfolds along the right, left, and middle line. There are many degrees to this path, and in each degree one gains egoism from the left line, and acquires altruistic balancing force (to correct the ego) from the right line. Our task is to coalesce the two lines in the middle, meaning use the ego altruistically.

Corresponding to those lines is a system intended to sustain them, like a rind that guards the fruit within it. For this reason, the system is named, "the *Klipot* (shells, peels) system." Its task is to guarantee the functioning of the lines.

The consequences of the work of the forces of the right and the left in the human society are Islam and Christianity, respectively.

The left and right lines help Israel keep a straight course in the middle line toward the realization of Nature's plan. During the exile, the force that operated on Israel came primarily from the left line. But toward the end of the correction of the collective human egoism, the right line is becoming increasingly active.

During the exile, the evolution of nations was characterized by the intensification of the egoism. Hence, the left *Klipa* (singular for *Klipot*) was the dominant force in designing the people of Israel and distinguishing it from the other nations of the world. It did that by hating Israel—that is, anti-Semitism. In doing so, it guarded the people of Israel from assimilating in the nations of the world throughout the centuries of exile.

However, since the end of the exile, this was no longer sufficient. Now the right *Klipa*, the force that stands opposite the balancing force, must be awakened and goad Israel to acquire the real quality of altruism.

Nature's inherent forces operate the elements in human society: the nations, the countries, and so on. Hence, since the time of Israel's exile, the left *Klipa*, Christianity, dominated our world. It took the place of Athens and Rome (which were not religions, or *Klipot*), dominated the world and suppressed all other methods.

But as the time approaches when Israel must correct itself and ordain the quality of altruism over ego, the domination of the force of the *Klipa* of the right is appearing in the world. This is what we feel today as a global intensification of the power of Islam over Christianity.

When the people of Israel begin to tackle the two *Klipot* and stabilize themselves in the middle line, they will encounter the *Klipa* of the middle line. It resides within them, in their own religion, and they will have to distinguish it, separate it, and uproot it from the world.

We should be aware that all the wars that Kabbalists describe can be decided at a higher level than the human-social level—it is the level of our desires. If we triumph there, succeed in realizing the correction method, and learn to use the ego altruistically, we will thus build the middle line. In that state, it will not be necessary for wars to materialize.

We should remember that the measure of balance or imbalance between Nature and us determines the corporeal, external reality, and the intensity of suffering we will experience. The key to the change is in our hand because the only active part in reality, for better or for worse, is the people of Israel.

INTERNALITY AND EXTERNALITY

Bear in mind that in everything there is internality and externality. Israel, the descendants of Abraham, Isaac, and Jacob, is generally considered the internality of the world, and the seventy nations are considered the externality of the world.

~Baal HaSulam,
"Introduction to The Book of Zohar"

The people of Israel are analogous to the key organs in the collective body of humanity—the brain, heart, liver, lungs, and kidneys—which operate the rest of the organs in the body. When these organs function incorrectly, the whole body suffers and grows ill.

Thus, the process of healing human egoism depends on the success of healing the people of Israel. The rest of the body will be healed by consequence, smoothly and easily. Because Nature's plan positioned the people of Israel to be in charge of the state of the world, we are considered the internality of the world, while the rest of the nations are considered the externality of the world.

In fact, whatever you examine, you will discover that it contains an internal part and an external part. The internal part in the object is called "Israel" and the external part is called "the nations of the world." For example, any person awakened to correct his or her ego, comprises two kinds of desires: Israel—the desire to achieve equilibrium with the altruistic Nature, and the Nations of the World—the egoistic desires.

Perfect balance with Nature is achieved only when all of one's egoistic desires are balanced with the altruistic Nature. It follows that everything in the world works in a similar manner. Thus, only when all people are corrected will we achieve the complete correction of human egoism. However, those who comprise Israel bear a decisive influence on the process, arising from the order of the correction rooted in Nature's plan.

When an individual from Israel raises one's internality, the altruistic desire, above one's externality, the egoistic desire, one strengthens the internality among others from Israel and in the nations of the world. In doing so, the people of Israel come closer to carrying out their task, and, as a result, the nations of the world will want to support and be closer to us.

If, on the other hand, one from Israel extols and appreciates one's egoistic externality above one's altruistic internality, that person raises the value of externality above internality on all other levels, too. In consequence, the people of Israel grow farther from carrying out their duty, and the nations of the world overpower us and degrade us.

This perception, which positions the individual from Israel as the designer of relations in the whole of reality, is expressed in Baal HaSulam's words: "Do not be surprised that the actions of one person bring ascent or descent to the entire world. ... Moreover, the parts compose everything that is in the whole." ("Introduction to The Book of Zohar," item 68).

In his book, *Orot HaKodesh (Lights of Sanctity)*, Rav Kook introduces a similar idea: "The magnitude of the value of man's power of will, and how crucial is his degree in reality, is yet to be revealed in the world through the secrets of the Torah (Kabbalah). And this revelation will be the crown of the whole of science."

Hence, although the people of Israel are few, they contain the necessary power and strength to carry out the required correction in the entire world. The awakening of the other nations depends entirely on the extent to which a person from Israel prefers internality to externality, or the Israel within over the internal nations of the world within.

Actually, the people of Israel determine the relationships between themselves and the nations of the world. The nations of the world are rising against us because we are empowering them. By increasing the importance of our egoistic part above our altruistic part, we are making the nations of the world overpower us on the outside, too.

If we could elevate ourselves even a bit toward equilibrium with Nature's altruism, our enemies would not want to fight us. And if we rose one more bit, they would become friends. It is a direct reaction, completely irrespective of them. We, in fact, operate them!

If we touched that intrinsic point, our enemies would immediately discover completely different desires within them, as if the day before had been erased. They would begin to feel that with our help, they could reach eternity and perfection.

Thus, to the extent that we disparage internality, humanity disparages us. If we extol the importance of realizing Nature's goal, humanity will regard us as the owners of the method that leads to happiness. This is the law of internality and externality, and it cannot be changed.

THE WAR OF
GOG AND MAGOG

The struggle between internality and externality is called "The War of Gog and Magog." It unfolds within the people of Israel, and its consequences determine the fate of the entire world. If we are triumphant, we will spare ourselves the horrifying depictions of the war of Gog and Magog as an apocalyptic global war.

The War of Gog and Magog is actually an internal war, occurring within individuals from Israel. It is not a physical war with planes and missiles, as is often thought. The planes and the missiles are not the real war; they are merely a physical manifestation of accumulated imbalance.

The war of Gog and Magog is a war between the internality and the externality of our desires. It is fought in our hearts and in our minds. As it unfolds, it gives us a choice. To which do we want to belong? Do we prefer the internality of the world or its externality? Where are our desires, minds, and hearts drawn? This is the war. And the purpose of this book is to make every person from Israel aware that his or her internality determines everything that happens in the outside world.

To win this war, we need a means that will increase the importance of the internality in our hearts. For precisely this purpose, the wisdom of Kabbalah has been revealed in our generation. Throughout our exile, which was both spiritual and physical, we have been disconnected from this wisdom. While a chosen few have been correcting their egos and perceived the inclusive Nature by using this wisdom, the rest of the nation has been completely detached from it, remaining with only superficial symbols of Israel's tradition.

We should be aware that the method for correcting the ego, which Moses gave to Israel—the Torah (Pentateuch)—was written in the language of the branches. It uses corporeal terms (branches) to point to spiritual elements (roots).

Kabbalists—people who have attained the comprehensive Nature and live in both the physical and the spiritual worlds simultaneously—know how to decipher the language of the branches. They identify to which spiritual root each corporeal branch points. Hence, they see the Torah as instructions for internal work in the three previously mentioned lines, which will correct the ego.

However, other people cannot see the language of the branches as anything other than corporeal depictions. They only see the superficial part of the Torah, and do not imagine that there is something hidden within it. Consequently, during the course of the exile, people began to treat the Torah as something superficial, like a history book or a legal constitution.

In "The Essence of the Wisdom of Kabbalah," and in *Talmud Eser Sefirot*, Part One, Baal HaSulam refers to this phenomenon as "materializing." He explains that it is a consequence of thousands of years of Israel's detachment from the spiritual world.

Until our time, Kabbalists kept silent about it. But when the immigration to Israel began, marking the end of exile, they emerged from hiding and called on the people to reacquaint themselves with life's purpose, which had been forgotten since the ruin of the Temple. They urged the people to use the wisdom of Kabbalah to that end.

Kabbalah is unique in the sense that it does not allow one to materialize, since the language it uses is not the language of the branches, but a "coded" language of worlds and *Sefirot*. It depicts all the elements of the ego and the phases to correct each of them in detail. Using graphs, charts, and calculations, Kabbalah leads the individual through the steps of the correction of the ego, points to the next step required at every stage, and explains how it should be done. It leaves no room for imagining that one can reach anything good in one's life without correcting one's ego. Finally, it shows that the way to achieve this correction is through internal, contemplative actions.

This is why Kabbalists explained that the people of Israel would regain equilibrium with Nature only through the wisdom of Kabbalah. This is also why they emerged to disseminate it to the masses. They realized that this was the only way the people of Israel and the whole world would come closer to redemption and deliverance from their adversities, as "this matter of the redemption… is the uppermost wholeness of attainment and knowledge" (Baal HaSulam, "Introduction to the Tree of Life").

The GRA (Vilna Gaon) wrote, "Redemption depends primarily on the study of Kabbalah" (*Even Shlomo*,
Chapter 11, item 3). Rav Kook explained similarly: "The
great spiritual questions that were previously solved
only to the fine and the great, must now be solved, in
various degrees, to the whole nation" (*Eder HaYekar ve
IkveyHaTzon*). Likewise, Baal HaSulam determined ("Introduction to the Tree of Life") that "only through the
expansion of the wisdom of Kabbalah in the masses will
we obtain complete redemption." Hence, he wrote, we
are obliged to "compose books, to hasten the circulation
of the wisdom throughout the nation."

But the Kabbalists were met with opposition. Not all
orthodox leaders joined their call; some opposed it and
tried to impede the dissemination of the Kabbalah. This
reaction is a result of the people's spiritual exile over the
past two millennia. During the last, and spiritually lowest stage of the exile, people without spiritual attainment
became leaders of their people.

A clear example of this approach is the treatment
that Baal HaSulam received when he began to disseminate the Kabbalah among the masses. His task was clear:
"I find a great need to break an iron wall that has been
separating us from the wisdom of Kabbalah since the
ruin of the Temple to this generation. It lies heavily on
us and arouses fear of being forgotten from Israel." ("Introduction to The Study of the Ten Sefirot," item 1).

In an attempt to prevent the approaching Holocaust,
in 1933 Baal HaSulam published a series of treatises.

The first treatise stated that there would be fifty such treatises, and the title of the first essay in the treatise, *Time to
Act*, clearly indicated the author's intention. Two weeks
later, the second treatise was published—*HaArvut (The
Bond or The Mutual Guarantee)*—and following it came the
third, and last treatise, "The Peace."

Baal HaSulam's intention to disseminate the wisdom
of Kabbalah to the masses was disagreeable to some public leaders, and they halted the publication of these essays
to prevent the spreading of the wisdom. Baal HaSulam
was not the first Kabbalist to receive this 'treatment.' The
Ramchal, for example, who tried to awaken the people
prior to the end of the exile, suffered from a similar attitude to his attempts.

In *The Gates of Ramchal*, essay: The Debate, p.97,
he wrote: "Rashbi (Rabbi Shimon Bar-Yochai) had so
screamed about it, and calls upon those who engage in
the literal Torah, that they are asleep ... It is the fruit of
the exile that Israel, through our many faults, have forgotten this path and remained asleep, immersed in their
slumber, and paying no heed to it. ... Behold, we are in
the dark, like the dead in the world, like complete wall-
scraping blind."

The battle for disseminating the correction method
in to the public is the most important war in reality. Its
consequences are indeed grave, since delaying the distri-
bution of the method will make the internality unable
to overpower the externality within each person, in the
nation of Israel and in the entire world. It follows that

this balance of forces determines the kind of world we will continue to live in.

Thus, it has already been written in *The Book of Zohar*: "Woe unto those people ... that make the Torah dry, without the moistness of mind and knowledge. They confine themselves to the practical part of the Torah, and do not wish to try to understand the wisdom of Kabbalah. ... Woe unto them, for with these acts they make poverty, ruin and robbery, looting, killings, and destruction exist in the world." (*Zohar, Tikkunim, Tikkun* 30).

Rabbi Chaim Vital, the Ari's disciple and scribe, sorrowfully wrote about it in his Introduction to the Ari's *Tree of Life*: "Woe unto those people from the affront of the Torah. Undoubtedly, by engaging in the literal and in its stories alone, it wears its mourning clothes, and robes itself with a sack. And all the nations will say onto Israel, 'What is thy beloved more than another beloved, what is your Torah more than our Torah.' After all, your Torah is worldly stories of trivia, too.' There is no greater insult to the Torah than that. Hence, woe unto those people from the affront of the Torah. And they do not engage in the wisdom of Kabbalah, which gives honor to the Torah, for they prolong the exile and all the evils that come into the world."

After the Holocaust, from 1945 to his last day, Baal HaSulam was preoccupied with publishing *The Sulam Commentary on The Book of Zohar*. In the introduction to the commentary, he explained once more the urgent need to begin to realize the correction method: "Now it is upon us relics, to correct that dreadful wrong. ... Then, each and every one of us will be awarded the intensification of his own internality...That force will come to the whole of the people of Israel. ... Also, the internality of the Nations of the World, the Righteous of the nations of the world will overpower and subdue their externality, which are the destructors. And the internality of the world, too, which are Israel, shall rise in all their merit and virtue over the externality of the world, which are the nations. Then, all the Nations of the World will recognize and acknowledge Israel's merit."

THE FUTURE OF THE WORLD IS IN OUR HANDS

From what has been said in this part, it appears that the solution to the global crisis depends particularly on us, on each and every member of the nation of Israel. Not on the leaders, but on every individual.

Every moment that we are not fulfilling our role is costing us a great deal. The duty of the people of Israel is one that cannot be avoided or turned down. It also cannot be ignored.

It is like the biblical story of the prophet Jonah, who was sent to warn the residents of Nineveh about the danger they were facing. Jonah tried to escape from the assignment he was given, but was forced to complete his assignment.

The story of Jonah is a pertinent allegory to all of us. This is why Kabbalists instructed that it would be read every year on *Yom Kippur* (Day of Atonement), the day of introspection. It is a reminder of our duty.

Even if we want to escape our responsibility in countries overseas, it will not help. Just as the sailors on Jonah's boat sensed that he was to blame for the storm that was about to drown them, and threw him off the boat, today the nations of the world are sensing that we are to blame for the world's predicaments, and their pressure on us will increase rapidly. The murky reality we are in today could be only the beginning of what lies ahead.

We have built in Israel an artificial bubble, and we are living our daily routine in it. Some of us believe that we will be able to overcome our neighbors by military force or that we will someday make peace with them. Either way, the general atmosphere is, "It'll be alright." We are unaware of the lurking blow, and so we are carrying on with our daily lives.

For the time being, we are allowed to live in Israel, even though we are behind in carrying out Nature's plan. This state is similar to the one that existed prior to the ruin of the Second Temple. The signs of the ruin were there some seventy years prior to the ruin itself, as the people declined to the lowest degrees of corporeality—unfounded hatred. However, the Temple continued to stand for a while longer, and the people were not yet exiled.

At that time, the ruin had already occurred on the level of forces, but it had yet to materialize. It was "on delay" for several decades. Today, too, there is a delay, but it is so that we will perform the correction. As soon as even a few of us begin to "lean" toward carrying out our duty, the balance of Nature's forces will change. The beginning of the realization of the method to correct the ego will produce an immediate change in the entire world. It is not surprising that the whole world thinks that Jews are manipulating the world, that they have some secret that they are unwilling to share. It is true, and others sense it subconsciously.

When our thoughts are egoistic, we are ill-effecting the world. However, if we want change, altruistic thoughts will enable us to change the world for the better, at lightning speed. We have been "chosen" in the sense that within us are powers of thought and will, which, if used correctly, will allow us to change reality instantaneously. We must recognize that and thus "sentence the world to a scale of merit" (Talmud Bavli, Kidushin, 40:2).

Today, it is recommended that every person become acquainted with the principles of the correction method, try to realize them within his or herself and pass this knowledge on to others. When we read books related to the correction method, or encounter similar material presented on the Internet, or watch a video on that topic, it strengthens our internality. This will intensify the sensation that our own future, our happiness and the happiness of our loved ones depends solely on achieving equilibrium with the altruistic Nature, and this will make us aspire for it. By doing so, we will immediately change the course of our lives.

To summarize, we should be aware that we are a special people. Everything that happens to us happens because of us. There is no one to blame but us. No one determines anything for us, and there is no other nation in the world that completely determines everything that happens to it.

It may be hard to accept and to take in, but everything is in our hands and depends on us. We are the only ones that determine our fate, and the fate of the whole world.

NOTES

[1] World Health Organization, Mental health, Depression, http://www.who.int/mental_health/management/depression/definition/en/; WHO, Fact sheet: Mental and neurological disorders http://www.who.int/whr/2001/media_centre/en/. The data were taken from the WHO site, as well as from the site of Israel Ministry of Health, http://www.health.gov.il/download/mental/annual2003/p2-12.pdf.

[2] World Health Organization, Mental health, suicide rates per 100,000 by country, year and sex, http://www.who.int/mental_health/prevention/suicide//en/Figures_web0604_table.pdf

[3] Dr. Dalia Gilboa, chair of the Inter-Ministry committee for prevention of youth suicide, http://www.health.gov.il/pages/default.asp?maincat=10&catId=75

[4] The White House Office of National Drug Control Policy (ONDCP), Drug Policy Information Clearinghouse, Fact Sheet, March 2003.

[5] Published June 27, 2006, http://www.ynet.co.il/articles/0,7340,L-3267779,00.html. The full report is available at the U.N. web site, http://www.unodc.org/unodc/en/world_drug_report.html.

[6] Data is taken from http://www.divorcemag.com/statistics/statsWorld.shtm

[7] Publish in a Yedioth Aharonot newspaper article May 14, 2006.

[8] Kabbalist Rabbi Yehuda Ashlag (1884-1954) is known by the title Baal HaSulam (Owner of the Ladder) for a commentary on *The Book of Zohar* that he wrote, titled "The *Sulam* (Ladder) commentary." Baal HaSulam is considered the successor of Rabbi Isaac Luria (The Holy Ari). His method is unique in that it allows any person to internalize the origins of the authentic Kabbalistic knowledge, which the formers Kabbalists have left behind.

[9] Baal HaSulam, *Preface to the Wisdom of Kabbalah*, item 1. This quote is also available in M. Laitman, *The Science of Kabbalah*, 2005, Laitman Kabbalah Publishers, p. 87.

[10] Babylonian Talmud, Baba Kama, 45, 72.

[11] Published June 2006 in Science magazine. The research was headed by 2002 Nobel Prize laureate in economics, Daniel Kahneman.

[12] Baal HaSulam, *Talmud Eser Sefirot (The Study of the Ten Sefirot)*, Part One.

[13] For more on this, see Nedelcu's and Michod's essay, The Evolutionary Origin of an Altruistic Gene, published May 2006 in the Journal of Molecular Biology and Evolution.

[14] From the biological point of view, it is customary to define altruism as behavior that is beneficial to others, ostensibly

at the expense of the creature's own ability to survive and multiply. Several theories have been constructed to explain why animals behave in this manner, and we shall briefly review the leading ones. The theory of "Group Selection" asserts that altruism serves the good of the group to which an animal belongs, hence the specific animal is rewarded by it, too. The theory of "Kin Selection" explains that if altruism is turned toward the kin, which carry similar genes, it indirectly contributes to the survival of its own genes. The "Symbiosis" theory argues that altruistic behavior is based upon the particular animal being somehow rewarded for the act. The "Handicap" principle relates to altruism as the way in which a particular element expresses its uniqueness and qualities.

[15] Frans B. M. de Waal, *Good Natured: The Origins of Right and Wrong in Humans and Other Animals*, 1996, Cambridge: Harvard University Press.

[16] Prof. Theodore C. Bergstrom, *The Evolution of Social Behaviour: Individual and Group Selection Models*, Journal of Economic Perspectives. Volume 16, Number 2. Spring 2002: pp. 67.

[17] All references to *The Book of Zohar* relate to Yehuda Ashlag's *Zohar with the Sulam Commentary*.

[18] *Dopaminergic polymorphisms associated with self-report measures of human altruism: a fresh phenotype for the dopamine D4 receptor*, Molecular Psychiatry, April 2005; 10(4):333-335.

[19] Editor's note: Perception of reality is discussed extensively in the author's book, *Kabbalah, Science, and the Meaning of Life*.

[20] In that regard, it is recommended to read Rambam's description of this process in *The Mighty Hand, Laws of Idolatry*, Chapter One, item 3.

[21] A. Nebel, D. Filon, B. Brinkmann, PP. Majumder, M. Faerman, A. Oppenheim, *The Y chromosome pool of Jews as part of the genetic landscape of the Middle East,* The American Journal of Human Genetics, 2001, 1095-112:(5)69.

[22] http://www.makorrishon.net/show.asp?id=14018

[23]   http://www.nrg.co.il/online/11/ART1/486/489.html

[24] Editor's note: the practical implementation of the principles, as they are presented in Baal HaSulam writings, is explicated in Rav Laitman's book *The Last Generation.*

[25] http://www.nfc.co.il/NewsPrintVersion.asp?docId=33202&subjectID=1

FURTHER READING

Kabbalah Revealed: The Ordinary Person's Guide to a More Peaceful Life: This is a clearly-written, user-friendly guide to making sense of the surrounding world while achieving inner peace. Each of its six chapters focuses on a different aspect of the ancient wisdom of Kabbalah, illuminating a teaching that has too often been shrouded in mystery and misconceptions.

The first three chapters in *Kabbalah Revealed* explain why the world is in a state of crisis, how our growing desires promote progress as well as alienation, and why the biggest deterrent to achieving positive change is rooted in our own spirits. Chapters Four through Six offer a prescription for positive change. Therein, we learn how we can use our spirits to build a personally peaceful life in harmony with all of Creation.

Basic Concepts in Kabbalah: By reading within this book, one develops internal observations and approaches that did not previously exist within. This book is intended for contemplation of spiritual terms. To the extent that we are integrated with these terms, we begin to unveil the spiritual structure that surrounds us, almost as if a mist had been lifted.

Attaining the Worlds Beyond: This book is a first step toward discovering the ultimate fulfillment of spiritual ascent in our lifetime. This book reaches out to all those who are searching for answers, who are seeking a logical and reliable way to understand the world's phenomena. This magnificent introduction to the wisdom of Kabbalah provides a new kind of awareness that enlightens the mind, invigorates the heart, and moves the readers to the depths of their soul.

Awakening to Kabbalah: A distinctive, personal, and awe-filled introduction to an ancient wisdom tradition. Rav Laitman—a disciple of the great Kabbalist Rabbi Baruch Ashlag (son of Yehuda Ashlag)—provides you with a deeper understanding of the fundamental teachings of Kabbalah, and how you can use this wisdom to clarify your relationship with others and the world around you.

Using language both scientific and poetic, he probes the most profound questions of spirituality and existence. This provocative, unique guide will inspire and invigorate you to see beyond the world as it is and the limitations of your everyday life, become closer to the Creator, and reach new depths of the soul.

Kabbalah, Science, and the Meaning of Life: Science explains life's mechanisms; Kabbalah explains life's purpose. In *Kabbalah, Science, and the Meaning of Life*, the author eloquently introduces earthshaking concepts so even readers unfamiliar with Kabbalah or science can easily understand.

Kabbalah explains that we are all one soul, materialized in many bodies. Similarly, modern science states that at the most fundamental level, we are all literally one. Science proves that reality is affected by its observer. Kabbalah states that reality, and even the Creator exist only within the observer. If you're just a little curious about reality and life's meaning, this is your book.

The Kabbalah Experience: Never has the language of Kabbalah been as clear and accessible as it is here, in this compelling, informative collection. The depth of wisdom revealed in the questions and answers of this book will inspire reflection and contemplation. Readers will also begin to experience a growing sense of enlightenment while simply absorbing the words on every page.

The Kabbalah Experience is a guide from the past to the future, revealing situations that all students of Kabbalah will experience at some point along their journeys. For those who cherish every moment in life, the author offers unparalleled insights into the timeless wisdom of Kabbalah.

The Path of Kabbalah: "Thou shalt not make unto thee a graven image, nor any manner of likeness" (Exodus 20:3). This prohibition from the Bible is also the

basis of the Wisdom of Kabbalah. Kabbalists state that
there is no reality at all, but something called His Essence, the Upper Force.

As uncanny as it sounds, this notion hides in its
wings the very prospect of freedom, for every person, for
every nation, and for the entire world. The structure and
the perception of reality are the surface of this book.

But the story of humanity, or more accurately, of the
human soul, is the undercurrent that drives the reader
forward in this book. It is about you; about me; about all
of us. This book is about the way we were, the way we are,
the way we will be, and most importantly, it is about the
best way to get there.

The Science of Kabbalah: Kabbalist and scientist, Rav
Michael Laitman, PhD, designed this book to introduce
readers to the special language and terminology of the
Kabbalah. Here, Rav Laitman reveals authentic Kabbalah in a manner that is both rational and mature. Readers
are gradually led to an understanding of the logical design of the Universe and the life whose home it is.

The Science of Kabbalah, a revolutionary work that is
unmatched in its clarity, depth, and appeal to the intellect, will enable readers to approach the more technical
works of Baal HaSulam (Rav Yehuda Ashlag), such as *Talmud Eser Sefirot* and *The Book of Zohar*. Although scientists
and philosophers will delight in its illumination, laymen
will also enjoy the satisfying answers to the riddles of
life that only authentic Kabbalah provides. Now, travel

through the pages and prepare for an astonishing journey into the Upper Worlds.

Introduction to the Book of Zohar: This volume is a required preparation for those who wish to understand the hidden message of "*The Zohar*". Among the many helpful topics dealt with in this text, readers are introduced to the "language of roots and branches," without which the stories in *The Zohar* are mere fable and legend. *Introduction to the Book of Zohar* will certainly furnish readers with the necessary tools to understand authentic Kabbalah as it was originally meant to be, as a means to attain the Upper Worlds.

Wondrous Wisdom: This book presents the first steps, an initial course on Kabbalah, based solely on authentic teachings passed down from Kabbalist teacher to student over thousands of years. Offered within is a sequence of lessons revealing the nature of the wisdom and explaining the method of attaining it. For every person questioning "Who am I really?" and "Why am I on this planet?" this book is an absolute must.

ABOUT BNEI BARUCH

Bnei Baruch is a non-profit organization that is spreading the wisdom of Kabbalah to accelerate the spirituality of humankind. Kabbalist Rav Michael Laitman, PhD, who was the disciple and personal assistant to Rabbi Baruch Ashlag, the son of Rabbi Yehuda Ashlag (author of The Sulam commentary on The Zohar), follows in the footsteps of his mentor in leading the group toward its mission.

Laitman's scientific method provides individuals of all faiths, religions, and cultures with the precise tools necessary for embarking on a captivating path of self-discovery and spiritual ascent. With the focus being primarily on inner processes that individuals undergo at their own pace, Bnei Baruch welcomes people of all ages and lifestyles to engage in this rewarding process.

In recent years, a massive worldwide search for the answers to life's questions has been underway. Society has lost its ability to see reality for what it is and in its place superficial and often misleading concepts have appeared. Bnei Baruch reaches out to all those who are seeking awareness beyond the standard, people who are seeking to understand our true purpose for being here.

Bnei Baruch offers practical guidance and a reliable method for understanding the world's phenomena. The authentic teaching method, devised by Rabbi Yehuda Ashlag, not only helps overcome the trials and tribulations of everyday life, but initiates a process in which individuals extend themselves beyond their present boundaries and limitations.

Rabbi Yehuda Ashlag left a study method for this generation, which essentially "trains" individuals to behave as if they have already achieved the perfection of the Upper Worlds while still here in our world. In the words of Rabbi Yehuda Ashlag, "This method is a practical way to attain the Upper World, the source of our existence, while still living in this world."

A Kabbalist is a researcher who studies his or her own nature using this proven, time-tested and accurate method. Through this method, one attains perfection and control over one's life, and accomplishes life's true goal. Just as a person cannot function properly in this world without having knowledge of it, the soul cannot function properly in the Upper World without knowledge of it. The wisdom of Kabbalah provides this knowledge.

HOW TO CONTACT BNEI BARUCH

1057 Steeles Avenue West, Suite 532
Toronto, ON, M2R 3X1, Canada

194 Quentin Rd, 2nd floor
Brooklyn, New York, 11223, USA

E-mail: info@kabbalah.info
Web site: www.kabbalah.info

Toll free in USA and Canada:
1-866-LAITMAN
Fax: 1-905 886 9697